The collector's all-colour guide to

TOY
Cars

An international survey of tinplate and diecast cars, from 1900 to the present day

The collector's all-colour guide to

TOY
Cars

An international survey of tinplate and diecast cars, from 1900 to the present day

Gordon Gardiner & Richard O'Neill

a Salamander book

Published by Salamander Books Limited
LONDON

A Salamander Book

Acknowledgements

Published by
Salamander Books Ltd.,
Salamander House,
27 Old Gloucester Street,
London WC1N 3AF,
United Kingdom

© Salamander Books Ltd., 1985

ISBN 0 86101 210 0

Distributed in the United Kingdom by
Hodder & Stoughton Services,
P.O. Box 6, Mill Road,
Dunton Green, Sevenoaks,
Kent TN13 2XX

Designer:
Barry Savage

Photography:
Terry Dilliway
© Salamander Books Ltd.

Filmset:
Modern Text Typesetting Ltd.

Colour reproduction:
Melbourne Graphics

Printed in Spain by:
Printer Industria Gráfica SA Barcelona DLB 12080/85

In the preparation of this book we received the most generous assistance and advice
from many toy collectors. Without the help of the individuals listed below, this record
of the toy cars of the 20th century could not have been assembled.

Special thanks for making toys available from their collections for photography are
due to:

Geoffrey Baker,
Liss, Hampshire

Glen Butler,
Henfield, Sussex

David Chester,
Bognor Regis, Sussex

John Churchward,
London (Toys appearing on pages 40/41, 42/43, 44/45, 84/85.)

Chris Littledale,
The British Engineerium Museum, Hove, Sussex

Shaun Magee Pedal Car Collection,
Bishop's Waltham, Hampshire

Ken McCrae,
London

Ron McCrindell,
Sidmouth, Devon

Peter Moore,
Motor Book Postal Auctions, West Chiltington, Sussex

Clive Willoughby,
London

Contents

Introduction	6
Colour Catalogues from European Makers, 1940s-1970s	32
Packaging by Japanese and German Makers, 1950s-1960s	34
Packaging by European Makers, 1950s-1980s	36
Tinplate Cars by European and US Makers, 1907-1932	38
Tinplate Cars by European and Asian Makers, 1950s-1960s	40
Tinplate American Cars by Japanese Makers, 1950s-1960s	42
Tinplate Cars by European and Asian Makers, 1950s-1960s	44
Diecast Cars by Dinky Toys, Britain and France, 1934-1950	46
Diecast Cars by Dinky Toys, Great Britain, 1938-1948	48
Diecast Sports Cars by Dinky Toys, Great Britain, 1939-1960	50
Diecast American Cars by Dinky Toys, Great Britain, 1939-1959	52
Diecast British Cars by Dinky Toys, Great Britain, 1947-1962	54
Diecast American Cars by British and French Makers, 1955-1972	56
Diecast Cars by Dinky Toys, Great Britain, 1956-1972	58
Diecast Cars by British Makers, 1956-1976	60
Diecast Cars by Dinky Toys, France, 1949-1968	62
Diecast Cars by British and French Makers, 1950s-1970s	64
Diecast American Cars by Dinky Toys, France, 1950s-1960s	66
Diecast Cars by Dinky Toys, France, 1960s-1970s	68
Diecast Saloon Cars by Dinky Toys, Spain, 1970s	70
Diecast Gran Turismo Cars by European Makers, 1950s-1970s	72
Diecast Gran Turismo Cars by European Makers, 1960s-1970s	74
Diecast Cars by West German and Japanese Makers, 1980s	76
Large-Scale Diecast Cars by International Makers, 1970s-1980s	78
Diecast Rolls Royce Cars by International Makers, 1950s-1980s	80
"Models of Yesteryear" by Lesney, Great Britain, 1960s-1970s	82
Tinplate Racing Cars by European and Asian Makers, 1950s-1960s	84
Diecast Racing Cars by European Makers, 1934-1972	86
Diecast Racing Cars by European Makers, 1950s-1960s	88
Diecast Racing Cars by British and French Makers, 1936-1964	90
Diecast Racing and Sports Cars by European Makers, 1930s-1970s	92
Diecast Sports Racing Cars by European Makers, 1950s-1970s	94
Diecast Sports Racing Cars by European Makers, 1950s-1970s	96
Diecast and Plastic Cars by Super Champion, France, 1960s-1970s	98
Diecast and Plastic Cars by Super Champion, France, 1960s-1970s	100
Diecast Sports Racing Cars by European Makers, 1960s-1970s	102
Diecast Sports Racing Cars by Italian Makers, 1960s-1970s	104
Diecast Sports Racing Cars by European Makers, 1960s-1970s	106
Diecast Rally Cars by Solido, France, 1974-1981	108
Pedal Cars by British Makers, 1930s-1970s	110
Pedal and Powered Cars by British Makers, 1930s-1970s	112
Pedal Cars by British and French Makers, 1930s-1940s	114
Pedal and Powered Cars by British and French Makers, 1930s	116
Pedal and Powered Cars by International Makers, 1920s-1960s	118
Pedal Cars by British and French Makers, 1930s-1960s	120
Pedal and Powered Cars by British and US Makers, 1950s-1970s	122
Pedal and Powered Cars by British Makers, 1930s-1980s	124
Index	126

Introduction

It is most appropriate that this book should appear in 1985, the year which, it is generally agreed, marks the centenary of the car as we know it; that is, a road vehicle powered by a petrol-driven internal combustion engine. From the time, a century ago, when the products of such pioneers as Benz and Daimler first rumbled along the public roads (in the early days, preceded by a man with a red flag!), the car has been a major preoccupation of a large proportion of the population of the developed countries.

Toymakers were quick to take advantage of the fascination exerted by the car over so many of their potential customers—a fascination that extended far beyond the ranks of those who could, in the earlier period of the automobile industry, ever hope to own a real vehicle, and one that embraced adults and children alike. By the turn of the century, metal and wooden toys representing cars (and, of course, commercial vehicles, which are dealt with in our companion volume "Transport Toys") of all kinds were appearing in sizes ranging from the diminutive tinplate "penny toys" (so called because they were intended to sell for that sum or its local equivalent) to pedal-powered models (usually made of wood in the earlier days) large enough to accommodate a juvenile driver and passenger. By 1904-05, such famous toymaking

firms as Bing and Carette of Germany were beginning to make tinplate toy cars a significant part of their large output of toys of all kinds.

SCOPE OF THE BOOK

We shall return later to the history of the toy car and an account of some of its most notable makers. First, however, it is necessary to outline the criteria we

adopted in assembling the toy cars that appear on the photographic spreads of this book (*pages 32-125*).

Both of the present authors were concerned, one as co-author and the other as editor, in the production of an earlier Salamander publication, "The All-Colour Directory of Metal Toys" by Gordon Gardiner and Alistair Morris, which appeared in 1984. In

that book, the "classic" tinplate vehicles produced by such toymakers as Bing, Carette, Güntermann and Märklin, and, from a slightly later period, Citroën, CIJ, Kingsbury and others, were well represented.

Obviously, we wished to avoid, as far as possible, the duplication of material that we had already presented to the reader in "Metal Toys": and in this book, coverage of the "classics" has been limited to a single spread of colour photographs (*pages 38-39*). However, the strongest argument against the inclusion of a large number of classic tinplate cars in a book primarily intended for the novice collector of limited means was that the prices of these items have now generally risen to a level that puts them beyond the reach of the average collector. Depending on condition, an early tinplate car by a wellknown maker may now be expected to fetch anything between £1,000 ($1,200) and £10,000 ($12,000) at auction: the latter figure was approached on more than one occasion in 1984-85, when fine tinplate vehicles by such makers as Bing and Märklin came under the hammer at international auctions.

CURRENT PRICES

Even tinplate toys in well-worn condition (in our system of classification ranging from "good" to "play-worn"; see *page 19*) will now fetch very considerable prices. At an auction held by Sotheby's, Pulborough, in April 1985, the prices paid for tinplate toys included £620 ($745) for a "horseless carriage" in only moderate condition, made by Güntermann, Germany, around 1900; £340 ($410) for a Limousine made in 1912, "probably" by Carette, Germany, and in what was described in the catalogue as "generally distressed condition"; and, from the later classic period (1920s-1930s), £370 ($445) for a "crudely repainted" 5CV Clover Leaf Tourer by Citroën, France, and £360 ($430) for a damaged Alfa Romeo P2 Racing Car by CIJ, France (for a good example of this famous tinplate toy car, see the photograph on *page 8*).

Even the prices asked for the

Right: *Alfa Romeo P2 Racing Car by CIJ (Compagnie Industrielle du Jouet), France. Introduced in the mid-1930s, this is generally acknowleged to be one of the finest of all tinplate toy cars. It has a powerful clockwork motor and is fitted with operating steering. Although well-detailed, the example shown is a "third type" model dating from the mid-1930s: it lacks the starting-handle, brake drums and shock absorbers that featured on earlier models. It is in fine condition and in its original finish. Although not particularly rare, these cars fetch high prices. Length: 20·86in (53cm).*

tinplate cars made in the 1950s-1970s by Japanese makers are now going beyond the resources of many collectors, with good examples approaching or exceeding three-figure sums. However, since many of these most attractive cars may still be obtained without the aid of an overdraft, we have included four spreads of modern tinplate cars (*pages 40-41, 42-43, 44-45* and *84-85*) which were most kindly made available to us by the notable London collector and dealer John Churchward.

As a result of the escalating prices of tinplate toy cars, most new collectors, for whom this book is primarily intended, are turning their attention to diecast models, and in particular to the diecast models of more recent years.

Therefore, the greater part of this book is given over to diecast cars, ranging from the pre- and post-World War II products of Dinky Toys (still the most popular with collectors) to models by such leading makers as Lesney (Matchbox), Corgi and Tri-ang (Spot On) of Great Britain, Solido and Norev of France, Mercury and Politoys (Polistil) of Italy, Tekno of Denmark, Mattel of the USA, and others. Again, we have tried to avoid unnecessary duplication of models that were shown in "Metal Toys".

PEDAL CARS

No book on toy cars would be complete without coverage of pedal cars, although the collector of these

fascinating vehicles will have to contend with both high prices (for restoration, as well as initial purchase) and the problems of storage and display of models up to around 6ft (2m) in length. But pedal cars were too attractive to be omitted, especially because, as in the production of "Metal Toys", we were given free access to the magnificent collection assembled by Shaun Magee at Bishop's Waltham, Hampshire. There can be no doubt that the major exhibition of pedal cars (including many items from Shaun's collection) at the National Motor Museum, Beaulieu, Hampshire, in 1983-84 considerably stimulated interest in this branch of the toy collecting hobby. Many unfamiliar models are shown on *pages*

Above: *A selection of cars from the "Minic" range of small tinplate clockwork-powered vehicles made by Tri-ang (Lines Brothers Ltd), Great Britain, from the mid-1930s until the 1950s. Shown here are (left to right; top to bottom): Rolls Royce; Vauxhall Town Coupé (note the most attractive original box); Ford Saloon (two versions; the lower one has a petrol can on the running-board, marking it as a pre-War model); Vauxhall Cabriolet; Caravan; Vauxhall Tourer; Bentley.*

110-125, along with some originally shown in "Metal Toys".

PACKAGING AND CATALOGUES

Our coverage is completed by one spread showing manufacturers' catalogues (*pages 32-33*) and two spreads on which packaging is illustrated (*pages 34-35* and *36-37*). Makers' catalogues, now increasingly hard to find, are both attractive in their own right and also an invaluable aid to in-depth research on models. And although some collectors and dealers may feel that "the box" has become something of a fetish and has made yet another contribution to the rising cost of collectable toys, it remains true that possession of the original box or

packaging will, in many cases, add significantly to the value of any model on the collector's market.

BEGINNING TO COLLECT

In spite of our somewhat minatory remarks on rising prices, we hope to convince the reader that it is neither difficult nor, necessarily, expensive to build up a satisfactory collection of toy cars—especially if some thought is given to the hobby before embarking on a series of purchases.

If you are new to the collecting hobby, you must begin by deciding just what kind of material you hope to collect. (Although our remarks are specifically aimed at the collector of toys cars, much of what we have to say is applicable to the collection of toys of all kinds.)

You must first consider how much money you can devote to your hobby. Obviously, unless your financial resources are near-limitless, you will not decide on the collection of classic, or possibly even more modern, tinplate cars. Nor, unless you have both large amounts of spare cash in your pockets and several spare rooms at your disposal, will you choose to specialise

in pedal cars. You are, therefore, most likely to decide on the collection of diecast models. (It should be noted that the collection of plastic models, either ready-assembled or built from kits, is outside the scope of this book; however, a few plastic-bodied metal-based cars will be found on the photographic spreads, along with a rather larger number of metal-bodied, plastic-based examples.)

The advantages of collecting diecast cars are many. They are fairly easily available: since the high original cost of mould-making for individual models had to be recouped, they were usually produced in large numbers. They are durable, and are thus more likely to be found in good structural condition (with a few exceptions, detailed below) than the more vulnerable tinplate toys. They are generally smaller than tinplate cars, and are therefore much easier to store or display. They are cheaper and simpler to restore, if in very rough condition, than tinplate cars.

And, of course, diecast cars are much cheaper to acquire than tinplate models: with certain exceptions (again noted below), the most sought-after diecast cars, those made by Dinky Toys between 1934 and 1940, currently fetch prices of between £25 ($30) and £300 ($360), with the majority tending towards the bottom of this range, while post-War Dinky Toys fetch prices ranging from around £20-£30 ($25-$35) for models dating from the later 1940s to as little as £3 ($4) and upwards for models dating from the 1960s-1970s. Unlike tinplate toys, diecast models remain in large-scale production, and many attractive and collectable diecast cars are currently in production and are available at prices ranging from about 75p (90c) to £15 ($18), for large and detailed models, in toyshops and model shops all over the world.

FINDING A THEME

Just about every type of car that has ever rolled off a production line in real life over the last eighty or so years is represented by a diecast model from at least one toymaker—and models of some famous types, such as the Rolls Royce Silver Ghost, the Ford Model "T", the Mercedes 300 SL and the Jaguar "E" Type, seem to have been produced by almost every maker in a bewildering number of variations. Thus, the range of potential collectables is immense, and if the novice collector is not to become hopelessly confused he will be well advised to choose a theme before ever he buys a model.

Although the exigencies of assembling material for photography have not always allowed us to be as consistent in this matter as we would have wished, we have attempted a broadly thematic presentation of the cars shown in this book. But our thematic divisions, basically between saloons and touring cars, sports cars, sports racing cars and racing cars, with further sub-divisions for individual makers, although suitable for visual presentation, are far too wide-ranging to serve as a guide to themes for the average collector. After all, we were able to draw our material from a number of extensive and long-established collections: the beginner will need to select a much narrower field.

MUSEUMS AND TOYSHOPS

A visit to to a museum may be productive of initial ideas for a theme. Most major museums in Europe and the United States now have on display toys of the past century, and there is a growing number of museums devoted exclusively to toys both ancient and

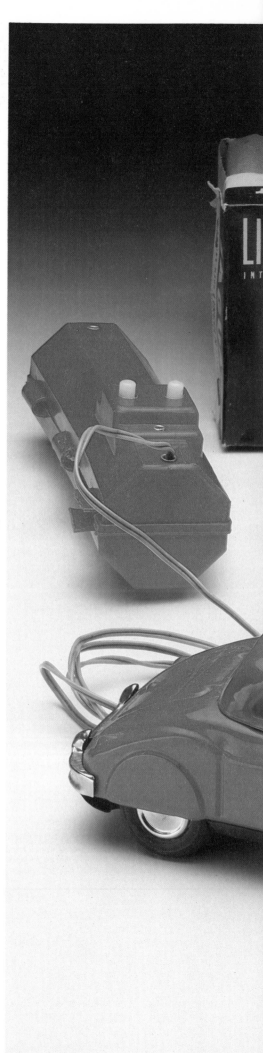

Above: *Novelty Veteran Car by an unidentified Japanese maker, dating from the late 1960s-early 1970s. The car is tinplate, with plastic seats and other details; the plastic figure of the driver appears to operate the steering tiller as the battery-powered vehicle moves along. Novelty toys of the "classic" tinplate period are now both rare in good condition (since they tend to be fragile) and expensive, but their Far Eastern-made equivalents are increasingly collectable and often feature ingenious mechanisms.*

Right: *Two Remote-Control Jaguar Cars by Lincoln International, "Empire Made" (presumably Hong Kong). Dating from the 1960s, these are lightweight tinplate toys of the kind that are now, as the prices of "classic" tinplate items rise, increasingly attracting the attention of collectors. The plastic hand-sets house batteries that power the rear wheels; the red plastic roof-lights flash and a siren sound is produced as the cars move. The plastic wheels have metal discs and rubber tyres. Length: 6in (15·24cm).*

modern. In Great Britain, a major collection of model cars is on permanent display at the London Toy and Model Museum, where many of the best diecast and tinplate cars are to be seen, while other fine specimens (with the emphasis on classic tinplate models) are to be found in the Bethnal Green Museum of Childhood, London, and the Museum of Childhood, Edinburgh. Large toyshops will generally have on display a wide range of currently available diecast cars, while more specialised model shops often have for sale a number of older models, either mint or second-hand. In the latter case, the novice collector can obtain some idea of the kind of prices now commanded by models that are no longer generally available.

SPECIALISATIONS

Following your initial research, you may be ready to decide upon a theme. You may conclude that you will specialise in one kind of car: saloon, convertible, sports, sports racing, racing; in cars of one particular marque; or in the products of an individual maker. But having made this decision, you must proceed to narrow down your field still further.

You have decided to specialise in one particular kind of car? Remember that there are hundreds, even thousands, of models of each type, and try to fix upon a single period and nationality.

You have decided upon a collection of cars of one particular marque? Then remember that the more popular the marque, the wider will be your field of choice: if you decide on, say, Hillman, Oldsmobile or Delahaye, you may end up with a most interesting, but small and laboriously-assembled collection; choose Ford, Mercedes or Citroën, and you could have a warehouse-full of models in a very short time.

You have decided to collect the products of an individual maker? Then remember that more than 1,000 Dinky Toys (not counting colour and casting variations) were issued, many of them cars, and that other makers—Corgi, Lesney, Solido, Märklin, Mattel—have been hardly less prolific. You will need to permutate all three possible areas of specialisation we have outlined.

Let us give a single example of the form your deliberations may take. Suppose your taste is for saloon cars: narrow this down to British saloon cars of a single period, say the 1960s. The marque you favour is Ford: so you will collect models of saloon cars made by Ford of Britain in the 1960s. By which maker? Find one of the increasing number of reference books now available, preferably one with an extensive check-list of models (a number of useful publications of this kind are

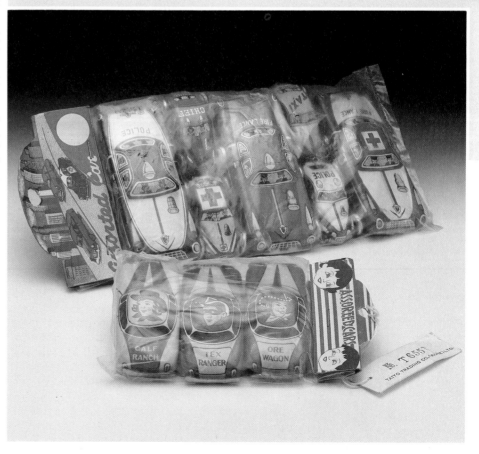

Above: *Steam Roadster by Mamod, Great Britain; modelled on a car of pre-World War I vintage, this splendid toy first appeared in the 1970s. Note the brass fittings — including radiator, carriage lamps, operating steering wheel and brake lever — the chromed bonnet and the spoked wheels with solid rubber tyres. The tray in the foreground holds the solid-fuel tablets used to heat the boiler: Mamod switched to solid-fuel firing in the mid-1970s.*

Left: *Two packets of "Assorted Cars" by Taiyo, Japan. Dating from the 1960s, when they were exported in great numbers (note the maker's consignment label on the three-pack), these brightly-printed cars in lightweight tinplate are the modern equivalent of "penny toys". Whether they will, in time, become as collectable and as highly valued as their diminutive forerunners remains to be seen; meanwhile, the collector should not ignore them.*

listed at the end of this introduction) and ascertain which makers produced models of the kind you desire. Result: you find that you can collect models made by Dinky Toys, Corgi Toys and Lesney (Matchbox Series), all of whom produced a fair number of models of British-built Ford saloons of the 1960s. You will also find that a few models that will fit into your collection were made by Tri-ang (Spot On) and Lone Star (Impy) of Great Britain, Solido of France, Politoys (Polistil) of Italy and Gamda of Israel.

This is, of course, just one possible field of specialisation. Your choice might equally well be to collect sports cars of the 1930s, American convertibles of the post-World War II period, sports

racing cars of the 1960s, Grand Prix racing cars of the 1950s, or any one of a score of other alternatives.

We recommend this thematic approach as by far the most interesting and flexible: in our " Ford saloon" example, you could, once your collection of British-made Fords is well-established, widen your scope to take in European-built Fords of the same period, thus adding Gama and Märklin of Germany, Tekno of Denmark and Best Box and Lion-Car of Holland to your list of makers, or American-built Fords, thus bringing in such makers as Hubley and Mattel of the USA and Cherryca Phenix and Diapet of Japan. Other wellknown marques would permit equal flexibility in collecting.

SERIES COLLECTING

An alternative to thematic collecting is to attempt to collect all the models in a single series issued by an individual maker. This might result in the formation of an exciting and valuable collection: it may also prove to be both frustrating and expensive. We draw only on British-made series for the examples given below.

Let us suppose that you decide to collect the sports cars of Dinky Toys "38 Series". Research will show that this series consisted of only six cars—the Frazer-Nash B.M.W. Sports Car (see (10-12), *pages 50-51*); Sunbeam-Talbot Sports Car (see (5-7), *pages 50-51*); Lagonda Sports Coupé (see (3-4), *pages 50-51*); Alvis Sports Tourer (see (8-9), *pages 50-51*); Triumph Dolomite Sports Coupé (see *Inset, pages 50-51*); Jaguar Sports Car (see (13-15), *pages 50-51*)—all of which were announced in "Meccano Magazine" as available from August 1938.

However, only three of these cars—the Frazer-Nash, Sunbeam-Talbot and Alvis—were, in fact, issued before production was ended by World War II in 1940; one of the models announced in the original series, the Triumph Dolomite, never appeared at all—it was replaced in the series in 1946 by the Armstrong-Siddeley Coupé (see (1-2), *pages 50-51*)—and the example we show, page reference above, is a modern copy based on Dinky Toys' original plans. It is almost impossible (some collectors would say that it is completely impossible) to distinguish between models in the series made before and after World War II, and various colour and casting variations mean that more than twenty examples would be required for comprehensive coverage of the series. Finding all of these in reasonable condition would be a long, hard task—and prices for individual models in the Dinky Toys "38 Series" currently stand at between

£20 ($25) and £50 ($60) each.

Admittedly, this is a fairly extreme example of the difficulties of series collecting—although some other early Dinky Toys' series would prove even more expensive and difficult to find. However, if we turn to a somewhat less rare and equally collectable series, Tri-ang's Spot On models (see *pages 92-93*), issued between 1959 and 1966, we face the problem of the extent of the series: around 60 cars were issued in the Spot On series (individual models, taking no account of variations), and they now attract prices of between £15 ($18) and £60 ($70) each.

CHEAPER ALTERNATIVES

Looking for a cheaper alternative, we can consider Lesney's "Matchbox 1-75" series. Most of the earlier, metal-wheeled examples are still obtainable at prices below £10 ($12) each (and the majority do not even approach that price), but these diminutive toys in

Above: *Ford Zephyr Saloon with Caravan; diecast models by a British maker, dating from the late 1950s. This set by a minor maker is in approximately 1:43 scale. Lacking all but the most basic details, it is diecast throughout, including the wheels and the base plate of the caravan.*

Left: *Ford Taunus 17M Station Wagon by Gama, West Germany. Dating from the early 1960s, this friction-powered toy was produced during the period when Western makers were increasingly turning from tinplate to plastic fabrication: the car has a tinplate base, but its body and wheels are plastic.*

widely-varying scales do not appeal to all collectors. The series is, in any case, far stronger in commercial vehicles than in cars. Lesney' Matchbox "Models of Yesteryear" series, see *pages 82-83*, is justly popular; although, as with the "1-75" series, the commercial vehicles are perhaps of greater appeal to collectors than the cars.

Perhaps more attractive to the series collector is Corgi Toys' series of racing, rally and speed cars, issued from 1957 onward and now comprising more than 100 models (not counting variations), many of them currently available from toy and model shops, with more still to come (after financial problems in 1984-85, Corgi has recently returned to production). Top prices for these models do not yet go above £20 ($25), even for the earlier, rarer examples. Corgi's "Cars of the 50's" series is well worth the attention of the collector of limited means. At the time of writing, fewer than 20 had appeared in

this most attractive series—featuring such cars as the Ford Thunderbird, Mercedes 300 SL/SC and Jaguar XK 120—and all were either current or easily available.

ACQUIRING MODELS

Let us assume, now, that you have decided on an area of specialisation and that you are ready to begin buying models.

As noted above, some very collectable toy cars are currently available in toy and model shops, and these will present few problems other than that of sticking to your budget. The location of older, scarcer models will require rather more effort. (Note that most of the information offered in this section applies equally to tinplate or diecast models).

Watch the "For Sale" advertisements in your local newspapers—and remember that other collectors will be watching them too, so you will need to move fast if a bargain seems to be on offer! Watch out, also, for notices of house clearance sales, usually organised by local estate agents: tinplate and early diecast models may sometimes be acquired as part of mixed lots of "toys", along with a fair admixture of junk. If you are an optimist, you will frequent jumble sales, although the toys to be found there have usually crossed the "play-worn" barrier to reach the "scrap-metal" category! Try putting your own advertisements in the local press, but be prepared to be

polite to vendors offering battered plastic-kit models or windowless, wheel-less wrecks at ridiculous prices: everyone now knows that "old toys" may be valuable; unfortunately, many non-collectors seem to equate poor condition with age.

Although you are not so likely to locate amazing bargains, the specialist press may be more rewarding. Hobby magazines tend to come and go, so watch your local newsagent's counter, and make a point of buying such hardy perennials as "Modellers' World" and "Exchange and Mart" (which has a special "Toys" section) in Britain, or "Antique Toy World" in the United States. Specialist magazines for car buffs also often carry features and advertising relating to models. And in the specialist publications you will also find advance notices of "auto-jumbles" and "swap-meets".

AUTO-JUMBLES AND SWAP-MEETS

An auto-jumble, as its name suggests, is a bring-and-buy sale organised by and for car enthusiasts. Since many motor buffs, although not toy collectors, often like to buy models of their favourite marques or of their own cars, there will usually be a few model dealers in attendance, while the "jumble" stalls themselves may have models for sale. Be warned, however, that at these venues, where non-professional dealers predominate, there is a chance that the prices asked will be

higher than those that would be expected from a specialist dealer or a knowledgeable collector. Non-professional vendors, sometimes inspired by an imperfect understanding of "price guides" (see our remarks on *page 18*), will often tend to over-value their stock.

More expert judgement of values is likely to be encountered at swap-meets, which are organised by members of the collecting fraternity in order to buy, sell or exchange toys among themselves. You may not find bargains—although it is surprising how often one collector's "rubbish" will prove to be just what another collector was looking for—but you will learn a great deal from just looking and listening. And if you do buy, prices will at least be fair (although, as in any field of human commerce, *caveat emptor* is the rule; so always examine any potential purchase very carefully, and never be afraid to bargain!).

DEALING WITH DEALERS

It is becoming increasingly common for model shops to run a second-hand dealership along with the marketing of current models, and there are, of course, many dealers who specialise in old toys either exclusively or as part of a general antiques business. Dealers are in business to make money and, since they often have to cover considerable overheads beyond the cost of their stock—rent of shop, advertising, employing help, and so on—their prices cannot be low: a dealer's "mark-up", that is, the price he asks for an item above what he himself paid for it, may be anything from around 20 per cent on an expensive but unpopular model to 100 per cent or more on an item which is not particularly valuable but is very much in demand. However, a dealer without regular customers will not stay long in business, so sharp practice, which may work once but is

guaranteed to drive away customers in the long run, and rank profiteering, are much rarer than is popularly supposed.

Do your best to find an expert dealer, perhaps through recommendations by fellow-collectors, and to establish a good relationship with him. An initial purchase, not necessarily of a rare or expensive item, should give you the chance to ask for advice on any similar models that may be available. If you seem likely to become a regular customer, plenty of good advice will be forthcoming; and once you are recognised as a serious collector, even if not a big spender (speaking from personal experience, we can say that most dealers value a modestly-spending *regular* customer more highly than the occasional plutocrat), it may well be that interesting items will be reserved for your first refusal and that part-exchanges for your unwanted or duplicate models may be arranged.

BUYING AT AUCTION

Having begun your collection with models purchased from dealers, from fellow-collectors at swap-meets and from similar "private" sources, you will probably sooner or later think of buying (or selling) at auction. The major international auction houses, such as Sotheby's, Christies and Phillips, now regularly mount special toy sales in which model vehicles are almost always a prominent feature.

The collector should not assume that because an auction house has a famous name, it is only interested in dealing with very valuable items: in Spring 1985, within a few weeks of putting a painting that brought bids of up to £8 million under the hammer, Sotheby's held a toy sale in which the prices fetched by lots containing diecast cars ranged from £18 ($22) to around £300 ($360). (It is worth noting here that at that same sale a single Dinky Toy

model—the Leyland Octopus Wagon, Dinky Supertoys Number 934, available from 1954 to 1964—offered in near mint condition and in a most unusual colour variation, fetched a price of £820 ($984); we believe this to be a record for a post-War diecast model.)

If you are at all nervous about venturing on to the auction circuit, remember that the auction houses are always willing to give advice on their buying and selling procedures. And even if you never make a purchase or a sale, attending as many auctions as possible will help you to obtain a good knowledge of current values of model cars and toys of all kinds.

For most auctions of any size, an advance catalogue will be available at least a fortnight beforehand. This will contain detailed descriptions of all the toys on offer, together with the auction house's estimates of the prices the various lots are expected to fetch (for

Above: *Chaparral 2J Racing Car by Politoys, Italy. It dates from the early 1970s: the transfer "J. Stewart" refers to Jackie Stewart, a world champion racing driver of that period. This diecast model in 1:43 scale features opening doors and rear compartment cover, with a detailed engine. Models of this kind are often to be found at auto-jumbles. Length: 3·622in (92mm).*

Above left: *Ford Thunderbird Convertible (in box), Cadillac Convertible (left) and Mercedes Benz 300SL (right), by Lincoln International, Hong Kong. Dating from the 1960s, these large diecast models— each is 7·5in (19·05cm) long—are friction-powered. Only the body castings are metal: the bases, wheels, bumpers, radiators and interior details are plastic.*

Top right: *Isetta Velam Voiturette ("Baby Car") by Quiralu, France. This diecast model in 1:43 scale, with clear plastic windows and rubber tyres, appeared in 1958. The prototype dated from 1958, and a model of this kind, illustrating what was a comparatively short-lived fashion for "bubble cars", would make an interesting collector's item. Length: 2·622in (67mm).*

the benefit of those wishing to make postal bids). Obviously, it will be well worth buying the catalogue, which will cost you no more than the price of a current model, whether or not you intend to go to the sale.

VIEWING AND PAYING

If you are thinking of bidding at the auction, you must be sure to attend the "views": the times appointed before the sale when the forthcoming lots may be examined by potential purchasers. Even if you do not intend to buy, the view may give you the opportunity to see and handle rare items.

If you are buying, remember that items are bought at auction not only "as seen", but also "as catalogued". Thus, if you buy an item that proves to be not as described in the catalogue,

really desire—but, of course, these surplus models can form part of your stock at the next swap-meet.)

A reserve price (that is, a price below which the lot shall not be sold) is agreed between the vendor and the auctioneer, and the lot is then ready to be catalogued and put up for sale. The reserve price must be realistic, for if the lot does not reach its reserve and therefore remains unsold, a "not sold commission" may be payable by the vendor. You should note, also, that a successful sale will entail payment to the auction house by the vendor of a commission of around 10-15 per cent. (Conditions as described in the foregoing paragraphs will, of course, vary somewhat from one auction house to another; our remarks will hold good for most British auction houses.

Right: *Two diecast models in 1:43 scale of Matra Sports Racing Cars by Solido, France. These were issued after the marque's first and second placings in the Le Mans event of 1972: as the "tricolour" boxes show, the French maker's marketing made full use of the French cars' success! Well-detailed models like these are aimed as much at adults as children, standing between genuine "toys" and "collector's models". Lengths: (No "14") 4·134in (105mm); (No "15") 3·898in (99mm).*

Below: *Possibly the nucleus of a "thematic" collection: three diecast models of Volvo cars by Tekno, Denmark. The Amazon 122 S (left), maker's reference number (MRN) 810, was issued in 1957; the Amazon Estate Car (centre), MRN 830, was issued in 1961; the PV 544 (right), MRN 822, appeared in 1959. The two later models have jewelled headlights, detailed interiors and suspension. Lengths: (left) 3·937in (100mm); (centre) 4·016in (102mm); (right) 3·898in (99mm).*

you may ask to have your money refunded. Remember, too, when it comes to paying for a purchase, that many auction houses now levy a "buyer's premium" of some 10 per cent, to which Value Added Tax (VAT) must be added (in the United Kingdom).

SELLING AT AUCTION

Rare or unusual toys are probably better sold at auction than elsewhere, since in the case of the more speculative items this may be the only way of establishing their true value on the open market. In the case of cars, this will apply particularly to the classic tinplate items by less-famous makers. For the vendor of diecast cars, the only problem will be that of forming a satisfactory "lot".

Most major auction houses will accept for sale lots, ie, either single toys or collections, which they estimate to have a minimum value of around £50 ($60). (If you are buying, this may mean that you will have to purchase some models that you do not want in order to acquire one or two that you

PRICE GUIDES

What is an individual model worth? The answer is the product of an equation involving four major factors. These are, not necessarily in order of importance: condition; rarity; desirability; availability. Every collector must work out this equation in terms of his own speciality. However, as we have stated above, you will be able to get a good idea of current values in all fields by regular attendance at auctions. You can also send for the lists of models offered for sale by various dealers in the columns of the specialist journals mentioned above.

With the increasing interest in toy collecting, many reference books, some of them highly specialised and dealing with the output of one toymaker only, have been forthcoming from publishers all over the world. Side by side with these have come a number of quite specific "price guides".

These can be most useful—we ourselves are much indebted to the compilers of the admirable "Swapmeet and Toy Fair Catalogue of British

Die-Cast Model Toys" (listed, along with other recommended titles, on *page 31*) for some of the value judgements we have made in this book—but a word of caution is necessary. The information given in price guides must always be interpreted in terms of current market conditions.

It must always be remembered that the prices quoted usually refer to toys in at least "very good" condition, and that the prices are generally based on auction records. Prices at auction may vary widely in accordance with a number of imponderables: the venue, the presence or absence of major dealers and collectors, the "mood" of the bidding (it is not unknown for prices to go "over the top" because of excessive enthusiasm, "sale room fever", on the part of the bidders), and various other considerations.

For three important reasons, this book is not a price guide. First, it is intended for an international readership, and prices vary considerably from country to country in accordance with the popularity and availability of

models. Second, price guides fairly quickly go out of date (the best are regularly up-dated), and it is hoped that this work of colour reference may be of use to collectors of toy cars for many years to come. Third, this book is primarily intended as an introduction to the pleasure that can be derived from collecting toy cars, not as a guide to collecting for investment.

We have, however, attempted in the captions for many of the models to give some indication of the subject's comparative rarity in comparison with other models of the same kind (eg, when we say that a Dinky Toy is rare, we mean that it is rare in comparison with other Dinky Toys of the same period; and likewise for other makers).

CONDITION OF MODELS

Desirability of a toy car will, of course, depend on the taste of the individual collector. On rarity, we offer the guidelines outlined above. Availability the collector will judge from his experience of dealers, swap-meets and auctions. What of the fourth element of

the value equation: condition?

Although the collector must always endeavour to acquire cars that are in the best possible condition, it is inevitable that there will be times when a much-desired specimen is only available in less than perfect condition. This is especially the case with such items as pedal cars, which were meant for active play and usually took plenty of hard knocks. Tinplate cars are likely to suffer from both loss of parts and from corrosion, while some earlier diecast cars, both those of lead alloy and some zinc alloy (or "mazac") examples, may be subject to metal fatigue.

As a guide to potential purchasers, auction houses and reputable dealers usually grade the toys they offer in terms similar to those that follow.

Mint:

As new, in its original box (if a boxed item) and with the box itself in good condition. If the box or packaging is not in fine original condition, the description "Factory Fresh" is sometimes applied, rather than "Mint".

Very Good:

The toy shows slight wear, possibly with some damage or fading of its finish, but with all its parts complete and undamaged. It may or may not be in the original box or packaging.

Good:

A sound example of the toy, but with noticeable wear from handling and use, and lacking its original box or packaging.

Play-Worn:

As the term implies, this designates a toy which has seen considerable use: it may have damaged or missing parts and it may have been repainted. Unless it is a rare or much-desired model, the collector should consider carefully the price asked before deciding to buy a toy car in this condition, and should ask himself whether it will be possible for him to re-sell it, if he can subsequently acquire a better example, at a later date, or whether it may be suitable for restoration work.

RESTORATION

If you do decide to purchase a "play-worn" example of a rare toy, you may have it in mind to restore it as nearly as possible to its original condition. (These remarks, of course, apply mainly to tinplate cars, since apart from the fitting of reproduction parts, which are now available for Dinky Toys and some other leading makes, there is little to be done to restore diecast cars). There are even collectors whose main interest lies in restoration and who will purchase tinplate cars in well-worn condition simply for this purpose.

However, the average collector is best advised to entrust the work of restoration to a professional. The process will not be cheap but, properly carried out, it will enhance both the appeal and the value of the model; amateur restoration will generally add little to the appearance and will detract from the value of the toys.

If you envisage selling the car at some time in the future, it may be better to leave it unrestored, since many collectors will always prefer an unrestored item, however play-worn, to one far-removed from its original condition. As a rough guide, it may be said that in the case of a rare toy restoration—depending always on the amount of restoration and the quality of the work that has been done—may

reduce the value of the car by between 20-30 per cent. In the case of less important models, restoration may more than halve the value. However, this does not apply to pedal cars, which will almost always demand restoration.

How you choose to display your collection will, of course, depend very much on its size and on the amount of space at your disposal. Ideally, both tinplate and diecast cars should be displayed in glazed cabinets: on open shelves, they will gather dust and become unpleasantly grubby in a surprisingly short time. Regular cleaning will be necessary, but this must always be kept to the absolute minimum to avoid undue wear.

Diecast cars can be dusted or cleaned with a soft brush to remove dirt from their crevices, but greater care must be taken with tinplate models. If they become particularly discoloured by dirt, the tinplate may be cleaned with mild soap and warm water and a final polish given with good-quality car wax and a soft, dry cloth. The mechanism of clockwork-powered models should be kept very slightly oiled. Whatever the method of display, the cars should not be exposed to direct sunlight, which will cause paint finishes to fade, and they should be kept at an even temperature to inhibit metal fatigue: extremes of temperature may "wake up" unstable alloys.

A BRIEF HISTORY

We hope that the practical information given above will be of both assistance and encouragement, especially to the novice collector. Although the space at our disposal forbids a comprehensive account of a wide-ranging subject, we proceed now, again largely for the benefit of the novice, to a short history of the toy car which, as we mentioned at the beginning of this essay, has been in production just about as long as the real thing. We begin by looking briefly at the history of tinplate cars.

Although the toymakers of the earlier period, up to around 1920, were not much concerned with scale, the greatest among them, such as Bing, Carette and Märklin of Germany, produced tinplate cars which were fairly faithful representations of the more famous marques of the period, such as Mercedes and De Dion. These cars, now generally rare and very valuable even in less than perfect condition, often incorporated a wealth of detail: opening doors, headlights (sometimes oil-burning working models) and sidelights, glass windows, operating brakes and steering, tinplate or composition figures of drivers and passengers, and forward-and-reverse clockwork mechanisms. The same period saw the birth of motor sport, and toymakers were quick to realise the appeal that

Right: *Studebaker Coupé by Dinky Toys, France; French Dinky Toys No 24o. This was made at Meccano's Bobigny factory in 1948-49; the model originally appeared in Great Britain, as the Studebaker State Commander, No 39f, in 1940-41, and was reissued in 1946-49. The photograph displays the car's tinplate base plate, stamped with the words "Dinky Toys", "Studebaker" and "Fab En France Par Meccano": the British-made car's base bore only the maker's name and "Studebaker". Length: 4·05in (103mm).*

Below right: *Lagonda Sports Coupé by Dinky Toys, Great Britain; Dinky Toys No 38c. Although this "38 Series" model was announced in "Meccano Magazine" as available from August 1938, it was, in fact, not produced until after World War II, when it was available from April 1946 until 1950. Note that the headlights are separate castings: the model will quite often be encountered with these damaged or missing, and the plastic windscreen is also quite vulnerable. Length: 4·016in (102mm).*

Left: *A thematic group of Aston Martin cars; diecast models, dating from the late 1960s-early 1970s, by French and British makers. (Back) Aston Martin DB4 by Solido, France; (left, centre and front) Aston Martin DB5 Vantage by Solido, France; (right centre) Aston Martin DB5 Volante (No 110) by Dinky Toys, Great Britain; (right front) Aston Martin DB6 (No 153) by Dinky Toys, Great Britain. Note the many details that Dinky Toys now featured. Lengths: (Solido cars, each) 4·055in (103mm); (Dinky DB5) 4·37in (111mm); (DB6) 4·252in (108mm).*

the speed, thrills and noise of motor-racing would always make to children. Racing cars have been popular toys from the tinplate era to the plastic age.

Up to World War I, German makers led the world in the production of toy cars, but in the post-War period Germany's economic problems, combined with lingering anti-German feeling abroad, produced a temporary eclipse of the German toymakers' production and export trade, and a consequent increase in the production of toy cars by other European and American makers.

Among the makers of tinplate cars to emerge in the period up to 1930, the names of Wells and Brimtoy (later to amalgamate) and Tri-ang (Lines Brother Limited) of Great Britain; Rossignol, Citroën, Jep (Jouets en Paris; but called J de P, Jouets de Paris, in 1928-32) and CIJ (Compagnie Industrielle du Jouet) of France; and Buddy "L", Kingsbury and Structo of the United States are all worthy of special note by collectors of model cars.

Tri-ang, a name that features prominently in this book, was largely the creation of Walter Lines, who had entered his family's business as a maker of wooden toys before World War I and, according to his own account, spent his spare time in the trenches during the War in sketching designs for toys. After the War, he went into business on a larger scale with his two brothers, adopting the punning trademark of Tri-ang (three Lines!) and making toys at first in wood, then in metal and finally in plastic, with a notable range of pedal cars made from the 1920s to the 1960s.

CITROËN'S AIM

The Citroën company began to issue models of its own cars, for sale in dealers' showrooms as well as toyshops, in 1923. The company's aim was partly promotional: André Citroën is reported to have said that a child's first words should be "Mama... Papa... and Citroën"! The popularity of the well-detailed Citroën tinplate models had the effect of causing other toymakers to put less emphasis on purely visual appeal and more on accurate detail, making scale of increasing importance.

In 1927, construction kits were added to the Citroën range and in 1928 the company began to produce diecast models. By 1933 production had reached an annual level of 274,000 tinplate models and 576,000 diecast vehicles, but it quite quickly decreased after 1935 (although JRD continued to produce a limited number of Citroën toys until after World War II). Another major French maker of the period, Jep is best known for its series of saloons and touring cars which began to appear in the late 1920s.

In the United States, the name of Kingsbury, especially, stands out by reason of its prolific production and for the good quality and robust construction of its cars. The company went out of production during World War II, and it is now best remembered for its series of "record cars", showing the vehicles that competed for the world land speed record in the 1920s-30s: the Napier Campbell "Bluebird II" of 1928, Henry Segrave's "Sunbeam 1,000 HP" and "Golden Arrow", and several others.

It should be noted that an equally fine range of "record cars" was produced at the same period (some of the models being of the same cars) by the German maker Güntermann, for by the mid-1920s a number of German makers had succeeded in re-establishing themselves in world markets. As well as Güntermann such makers as Tipp and Bub were notable at this time, the latter taking over production of some items from the range of Carette, for that famous French-owned but German-based firm had not survived World War I.

TINPLATE UP TO 1950

Apart from Bing, which ceased production around 1933, most of the major makers mentioned above continued to produce toy cars in the period leading up to World War II. This decade was also notable for the emergence of a number of "construction kit" cars.

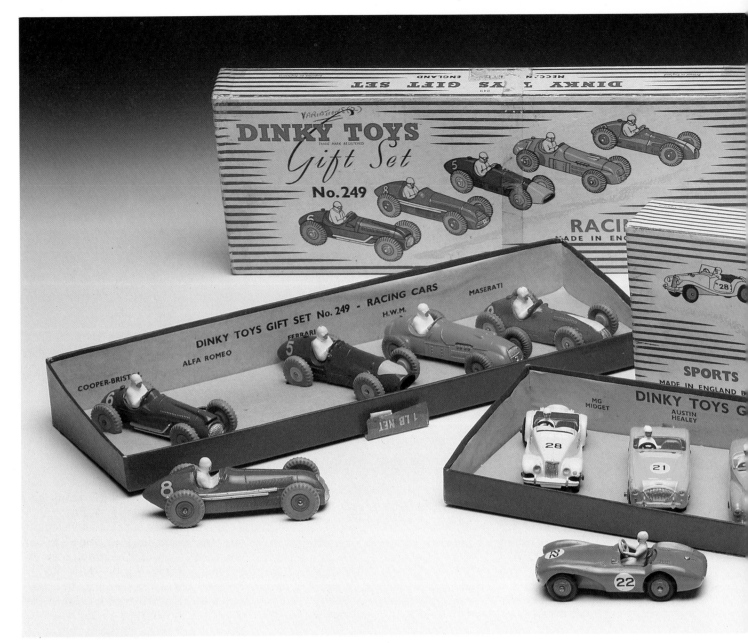

Citroën's entry into this field is noted above. Kits from which toy cars (or, less often, commercial vehicles) could be assembled by an older child were issued in Great Britain by Meccano and in the "Ubilda" range of Burnett Limited (later called Chad Valley), and in the United States by Structo, which, with its famous slogan "Structo Toys Make Men of Boys", reversed the construction process by marketing finished cars of nut-and-bolt construction that were intended to be dismantled and re-assembled.

In Germany, Märklin too issued construction kit vehicles, although German toymakers of the 1930s—somewhat forebodingly, one may say with hindsight—tended to concentrate their efforts on military vehicles and equipment of all kinds: Hausser, Lineol, Tipp and Arnold are especially wellknown for their production of tinplate military vehicles in the 1930s. The major maker of non-military vehicles at this time was Schuco, a firm still active in the production of ingenious mechanical toys.

After World War II, the production of tinplate toy cars by European and American makers continued on a reduced scale, the most prominent makers being Arnold and Schuco of West Germany (it is worth noting that German-made tinplate cars of the immediate post-War period will usually be found with the mark "Made in US Zone"), the Marx company of the USA, and Wells Brimtoy, Chad Valley and Mettoy of Great Britain.

THE ASIAN CONQUEST

From the 1950s, the centres of production for tinplate cars (and, indeed, for tinplate toys of all kinds) increasingly shifted to the Far East, particularly to Japan. Japanese toymakers had long been in production, of course, but it was only from around 1950 onwards, during the miracle of Japan's post-War reconstruction, that their marketing became so efficient and their prices so competitive that Western makers were unable to match them in the production of toys, as in a number of other manufacturing fields.

Faced with a diminishing market for tinplate toys—which were adversely affected both by the coming of plastic construction methods that allowed more detailed models to be more cheaply produced, and by increasingly stringent safety regulations that dictated standards for the construction and finish of tinplate toys that made them increasingly expensive to manufacture—western makers virtually abandoned tinplate. Japanese and other Asian makers, however, continued to produce tinplate cars of good quality, like those shown on four spreads in this book.

THE FIRST DIECAST CARS

Small toy cars made by the diecasting process have been on the market almost as long as tinplate models, for some "penny toys" were made by diecasting (although they were much more often of tinplate) from around the turn of the century. However, the diecast toy car as we know it today—a small model made by the pressure-casting of lead or, more usually, zinc

alloy; the latter material is generally known as "mazac" in the United Kingdom, and as "zamac" in France and the United States—did not really establish itself until the mid-1920s.

The first important name in the production of diecast cars is that of Tootsietoy (the trade-name of the Dowst company) of the USA. This maker began to produce diecast cars just before World War I, and by the mid-1920s had in production quite a wide range of cars and other vehicles in diecast mazac. A few French makers produced a small number of lead cast cars of a very fragile nature at around the same time, while Citroën, as noted above, issued lead cast (and, a little later, composition) models from 1928. Another fairly early maker of diecast cars in mazac was Manoil of the USA, whose limited range of vehicles in 1:43 scale (somewhat larger that those of Tootsietoy, which at first preferred 1:60 scale) included cars that were typically of "futuristic" shape and were fitted with wooden wheels.

These pioneers were soon followed by three of the greatest names in diecast car production, all of whom feature on the photographic spreads of this book. Meccano of Great Britain was active in the field from 1934 until until 1978; Märklin of Germany was active from 1936; Solido of France was active from 1938. The two latter makers remain in production—but of the three, it was Meccano, with its range of Dinky Toys, that was to become the best-known, the most prolific, and, to this day, the most eagerly collected all over the world.

MECCANO "MODELLED MINIATURES"

Meccano Ltd, the toy company established in Liverpool by Frank Hornby before World War I, originally concentrated on the production of the metal construction sets with which the Meccano name is chiefly associated. From just after World War I, clockwork and electric train sets were made under the Hornby name, establishing a dominant position in European markets (see Salamander's companion volume, "Toy Trains" by Ron McCrindell, for the Hornby story). In 1931, Meccano introduced "Modelled Miniatures", a series of cast metal accessories intended to complement Hornby train sets.

The earlier "Modelled Miniatures" sets, numbered 1-21, were of station figures, lineside furniture, agricultural equipment and the like. However, Set No 22, announced in the "Meccano Magazine" for December 1933, but possibly available a little earlier, consisted of six diecast vehicles in approximately 1:48 scale: a motor truck, a delivery van, a tractor, a

Top: *These Gift Sets issued by Dinky Toys, Great Britain, shown here with their boxes, would be a most valuable addition to any collection: both are very scarce. Gift Set No 249 (originally No 4), Racing Cars, was available from 1953 until 1955; Gift Set No 149, Sports Cars, issued 1958, was available until 1961.*

Above: *Dinky Toys, France, marketed its Citroën Presidentielle (No 1453), made in the early 1970s, in a stout presentation box. This impressive model of a Presidential limousine, complete with flag, features battery-powered lights, opening doors and boot, and a detailed interior (including driver). Length: 6in (152mm).*

Above: *Two versions of one of the most frequently-modelled cars: the Jaguar "E" Type. The XKE Convertible (No 926) by Tekno, Denmark, was issued in 1964 along with a model of an XKE Hard Top (No 927). It has an opening bonnet (with detailed engine), doors and boot (with spare wheel), and suspension. The Jaguar "E" Type (No 120) by Dinky Toys, Great Britain, available 1962-67, has a detachable hard top.*

Right: *Five models from the Spot On range, made in 1959-66 by Tri-ang, Great Britain, are seen here with a Dinky Toys contemporary. (Left to right; top to bottom): Bristol 406, Spot On No 115, 1960; Armstrong Siddeley 236 Sapphire, Spot On 101, 1959; Jaguar "S" type, Spot On 276, 1964; Vauxhall Cresta, Spot On 165, 1961; Jensen 541, Spot On 112, 1960; Holden Special Sedan, Dinky Toys 196, 1963.*

tank—and two cars, a Sports Car (later given the number 22a) and a Sports Coupé (later number 22b). These were cast in lead alloy (as were a few other earlier models in the range), and their comparative frailty has resulted in extreme rarity: a complete set is just about impossible to find, and individual models of the two cars now attract prices of around £300-£400 ($360-$480) each.

"DINKY TOYS" APPEAR

Perhaps in answer to the success of the Tootsietoy models that were then being exported to Great Britain, Meccano quite quickly decided to expand its range of diecast vehicles. By April 1934, the range had been renamed "Dinky Toys", the now-familiar reference numbers had made their appearance, and the emphasis had been moved from toy railway accessories to specifically automotive items. Among the models announced at this time were the Racing Car (Number 23a; see (1-3), pages 86-87), and the ambulance and seven cars that made up the "24 Series". Like the "22 Series", the cars did not represent any particular marque (although No 24d was called the "Vogue Saloon"). In 1938, however, the same body castings, with remodelled radiators and some other changes, were used for the cars of the "36 Series" (see pages 48-49), which were named for specific marques: the casting for the

Vogue Saloon, for example, was used for the Humber Vogue (No 36c; see (16-18), pages 48-49).

This is but one, early, example of the many stylistic variants (and later the complicated numbering and re-numbering of models) that fascinate the experienced collector of Dinky Toys but sometimes bewilder the novice. So complex is the subject, since more than 1,000 Dinky models (not counting variations) had appeared before the final closure of the Liverpool factory in 1979, that to attempt to deal with it in the space we have available would only serve to confuse the reader. Many of the more arcane points of casting and colour variation and numbering are dealt with in the captions to the several colour spreads on which Dinky Toys are shown: the reader will find more detailed information in several of the sources listed in our "Bibliography" on page 31 (the titles by Gibson, Ramsay and the Richardsons are particularly recom-

mended in this context).

By early 1936, some 200 Dinky Toys of various kinds had appeared from Liverpool and further items were appearing from the Meccano factory in France, at Bobigny, near Paris. Over the years, some French Dinky Toys were marketed also in Great Britain (a number are illustrated on the photographic spreads), and many collectors are of the opinion that the style and finish of the French-made cars is generally superior to that of models of British manufacture.

"FOREIGN" DINKY TOYS

Much later, in 1968, Dinky Toys cars were also made in Hong Kong: the "Mini Dinky" range, in 1:65 scale. A later Hong Kong-made series, dating from around 1980, consists of models much resembling the "Matchbox 1-75" range. Further models were produced in India from dies sold as obsolete by Meccano in 1968-70. These were marketed, in boxes almost identical to

those of the British models, as "Nicky Toys", although the bases of some are still to be found with the original Dinky Toys stampings.

With the exception of the French models, none of the "foreign" Dinky cars are, as yet, thought to be particularly collectable. Most collectors' interest centres on the models issued in Britain in the 1950s and 1960s, since these are still generally available at reasonable prices. Pre-1940 Dinky Toys, however, are generally both rare and very expensive—and great care must be taken if a purchase of a pre-War Dinky Toy is contemplated.

Because of the use, in the earliest models, of lead alloy, or of an unstable mazac mixture, pre-War models are subject to metal fatigue which may cause them literally to crumble to dust! A model with advanced metal fatigue is virtually unrepairable, but in the earlier stages, recognisable by a spreading network of cracks extending through the paint finish to the bodywork, metal fatigue may possibly be arrested by coating the interior of the car with resin adhesive.

RECOGNITION POINTS

The best advice for a novice collector who is offered a pre-War Dinky car, with or without packaging, is to inspect it very carefully for signs of repair and repainting. As well as having vulnerable bodies, pre-War models may have been fitted with new tyres, since the original tyres are likely to become soft and develop "flats" or to become brittle and crumble. Here, it is worth remembering that most (but not all) pre-War Dinky cars were originally fitted with white rubber removable tyres, while the tyres of most post-War examples were of black rubber.

Since many pre-War Dinky models were re-issued post-War, a few other recognition points for use in dating may be useful. Almost all Dinky Toys have the maker's name—either "Meccano Ltd", "Meccano Dinky Toys" or "Dinky Toys"—stamped on the metal base plate, but on most pre-War models the stamping does not include the name of the car itself nor the model number, whereas most post-War models have the model name or number, or both. Almost all pre-War models have smooth wheel hubs, sometimes with silver plating; most post-War models have ridged wheel hubs, which are never found with plating.

With a few exceptions, all models produced before the late 1950s have mazac wheels; polished metal wheels were fitted to some models issued thereafter, and later plastic and "speedwheels" made their appearance. Plastic windows were first fitted to Dinky Toys in 1958; suspension systems appeared in 1959; "fingertip steering" and detailed interiors were fitted from 1960; and opening doors, bonnets (sometimes with detailed engines) and boots, and jewelled headlights date from 1963. For details of the complex casting and chassis variations that

assist in dating models, the reader is referred to the titles in the "Bibliography" cited above.

TRI-ANG'S "SPOT ON" RANGE

As the reader may judge from the foregoing paragraph, the late 1950s and early 1960s saw a greater degree of sophistication in Dinky Toys cars. This was forced on the company by the activities of such British competitors as the "Spot On" range made by Tri-ang (Lines Brothers Ltd)—the firm that would, in 1964, take over Dinky Toys; the "Matchbox" and "Models of Yesteryear" ranges issued by Lesney; and the models produced by Playcraft Toys (Mettoy) under the "Corgi" trademark.

The cars of the Spot On range first appeared in 1959. Made to a scale of 1:42, somewhat larger than the standard Dinky cars, Spot On cars were distinguished by their truth to prototype. They were finished in the colour

schemes specified for the real cars, pictures of which were packed in each box, and featured from the outset such details as "independent" suspension, plated radiators, bumpers and hub caps, treaded rubber tyres, number plates, detailed interiors with seats and steering wheels, and plastic windows. Now highly collectable, Spot On cars are easily recognisable: all have the maker's name, model name and the scale stamped on the base.

CORGI THE INNOVATOR

Although Spot On models are probably a little more favoured by collectors, Corgi cars (the trademark stemmed from the Playcraft company's Welsh location) have great appeal and their maker deserves considerable credit for innovatory features.

Appearing from 1956 onward, at first in scales between 1:45 and 1:50 and from the 1970s in 1:42 scale, Corgi cars were from the outset fitted with

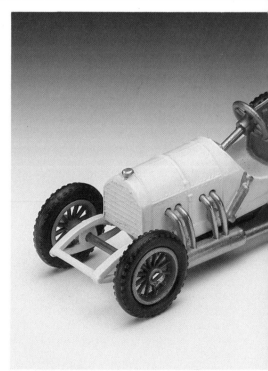

Above: *The Saint's Volvo P1800 by Corgi, Great Britain; maker's reference number 258, issued in 1965 and available until 1959. Two colour variations are shown: a later version, No 201, available 1970-72, was fitted with "whizzwheels" and lacked a driver. Length: 3·5625in (90mm).*

Left: *The two versions of the Austin A60 Motor School Car by Corgi, Great Britain. No 236 (left) was available 1964-69; No 255 (right) was available 1964-68. The significant difference is that No 236 is right-hand drive; No 255 is left-hand drive. Length: 3·74in (95mm).*

Below: *Three "First Issue" cars, all dating from 1958, from the increasingly-popular "Models of Yesteryear" series made by Lesney, Great Britain. (Left to right): 1908 "Grand Prix" Mercedes (Y-10); 1929 Le Mans Bentley (Y-5); Morris Cowley 1926 "Bullnose" (Y-8).*

clear plastic windows. Most earlier models have tinplate base plates bearing the maker's and model's names: diecast chassis with transmission and other details were introduced around 1960 and detailed plastic chassis were later fitted. In 1961, Corgi was able to claim that, as well as windows, it had been the first to fit such details as jewelled headlights and ruby rearlights, opening bonnet with detailed engine, opening boot with spare wheel, self-adhesive decals (for number plates, licence discs, etc), and full suspension and "fingertip steering".

Another aspect of Corgi's innovatory efforts is evident in the maker's mechanical experiments. A few of the earlier models, appearing before 1959,

were produced both in unpowered form and with friction-drive motors, but the latter were not very successful and were soon dropped from the range. The 1960s saw the introduction on some models of removable wheels ("Golden Jacks") and on others of ingenious "Trans-o-lite" working headlights.

In the 1980s, micro-chip technology was harnessed in the "Corgimatic" range of vehicles, with movement, working lights and engine noise: a model of the M.G. Maestro 1600 (Number C.1800) in this form was issued in 1983. The collectability of these advanced models remains to be proved by time; that of Corgi's fine "Cars of the 50's" series has already been noted.

"MATCHBOX" AND "YESTERYEARS"

Both the Spot On and Corgi ranges were preceded in production by the "Matchbox" series of Lesney, a company founded in 1947 (and trading until the later 1950s as Moko Lesney). The diminutive models in the "1-75 Series" (the first 75 models were numbered consecutively; thereafter, new models took on the serial numbers of those they were issued to replace) appeared from 1953 onwards. In various scales, ranging from 1:42 to 1:198 (the cars in the series generally falling into the 1:62/1:80 bracket), they were until the mid-1960s marketed in the matchbox-type containers from which they took their name. As the series developed, the boxes grew larger and more colourful: bubble packs were used from 1981 and window boxes, with slotted display tabs, for the

"1-75 Series" appeared in 1983.

All "1-75" models are stamped with the name "Lesney" and most bear also the model number and (post-1957) the model name. Most post-1965 issues also bear the word "Matchbox". The earlier models in the series, with metal wheels on axles with crimped ends, are most favoured by collectors; grey or black plastic wheels on axles with domed ends were fitted during the 1960s, and fat plastic "superfast" wheels appeared towards the end of that decade. Plastic base plates began to replace metal ones during the 1970s. Of other details, plastic windows were fitted from 1961 onwards and suspension was featured from 1965.

BEWARE OF FORGERIES

The vehicles in the Lesney Matchbox "Models of Yesteryear" range are far more popular with collectors than

Above: *Colour and construction variations occur on many cars in Lesney's "Models of Yesteryear" series. Shown here are (clockwise): 1929 4½ Litre Bentley (2nd Issue, Y-5), 1962 (dark green) and 1965 (red tonneau) versions; 1913 Mercer Raceabout (2nd Issue, Y-7), 1961 (lilac) and 1965 (yellow) versions; 1923 Type 35 Bugatti (2nd Issue, Y-6), 1964 (red) and 1961 (blue) versions. The colour change from blue to red on the Bugatti was a step away from realism: it normally raced in the blue colours of France.*

Above left: *Casting and tyre variations are illustrated in these two versions of the "Models of Yesteryear" 1907 Rolls Royce Silver Ghost (1st Issue, Y-15), issued in 1960. Note the cutaway area towards the rear of the running-board on the model in the background, and also the grey tyres that definitely establish this as the scarcer variant. The metal-spoked wheels are also of difference colours: silver on the background model, gold on that in front. The shades of metallic green on the main body of this car may vary slightly, but this is not intentional.*

those of the "1-75 Series". These handsome, well-detailed models of vintage and veteran vehicles first appeared in 1956: the earliest models were of commercial vehicles—see our companion volume, "Transport Toys" —and the first cars in the series—the 1929 Le Mans Bentley (Y-5), Morris Cowley 1926 "Bullnose" (Y-8) and 1908 "Grand Prix" Mercedes (Y-10), see photograph, *page 27*—were issued in 1958.

There have been four issues (ie, series within the major series) of "Yesteryears", the same numbers being used in each issue, and since some models from all four issues remain currently available (with new ones still appearing), only a detailed checklist will enable the collector to trace the course of the various issues and the many colour and minor construction variants. Of more than 60 "Models of

Yesteryear" that have so far appeared (not counting colour and construction variants), just over half are cars.

All have metal chassis, with all pre-1983 issues bearing the series name, the model's name and number, and the words "Made in England by Lesney". The scales, which vary widely—although most of the cars fall into the 1:40/1:55 bracket—are printed on the boxes, as are fairly comprehensive details of the prototypes, including engine capacity and other technical information.

"Models of Yesteryear" issued before 1970 have metal wheels; those issued in 1970-73 may have metal or plastic wheels, and thereafter plastic wheels are fitted, with treaded plastic tyres in all cases. Until the mid-1970s, such fittings as radiators, bumpers and headlights were all of metal; thereafter plastic was more often employed.

It is worth noting that there have been "limited" issues of some "Models of Yesteryear"—notably a variation in black finish with gold trim of the 1911 Model "T" Ford (Y-1, 2nd Issue), of which 1,000 only were made for sale by special order in the USA—and that forgeries of these rare models are known to have been offered for sale.

(It should be noted also that forgeries are known to exist of some of the rarer Dinky Toys cars—especially those models in which colour variations significantly affect the values. There is no simple guide to spotting such forgeries if they are well-executed: therefore, provenance will be of great importance in the case of very rare Dinky Toys models.)

DATING PEDAL CARS

A number of good reference books and check-lists exist to serve the interests of collectors of tinplate and diecast cars, and these may be used to supplement our necessarily brief and somewhat generalised guide to these collecting activities in this essay. The collector of pedal cars, however, is less well-served by reference material, and we will therefore conclude with a few notes on dating these "big brothers".

In the earlier period, do-it-yourself kits of mechanical parts were available to allow the competent amateur to construct a vehicle to his own design: in other words, in such vehicles the pedal mechanism, wheels, axles and steering may be standard, but the bodywork is a matter of individual taste and skill. Some most unusual vehicles resulted from such activities, and their very individuality should enable the collector to recognise them.

Whatever its construction—and, generally speaking, wood panelling is more common in earlier examples and metal in later ones—the best guide to the date of a pedal car is probably its drive. Examples dating from the years before and soon after World War I generally have chain-drive, with inch-pitch block chains (ie, block-shaped links with one-inch spaces) on earlier cars, and half-inch-pitch roller chains on the later ones. Crank-drive, cleaner and less likely to trap the hand or feet of juvenile drivers, gradually super-seded chain-drive.

The majority of early pedal cars have simple direct steering, but in the 1920s Ackerman-type steering—in which the length of the trackrod is less than the distance between the stub axle pivot points, causing the inner wheel on the turn to describe a tighter arc than the outer—became more generally used. The wheels of earlier cars are usually radially-spoked; tangentially-spoked wheels came later, giving way in their turn (rather as in real cars) to "easy-clean" disc wheels.

On cars made from around 1930 onward, wheel bearings and axle bearings may be fitted: plain bearings at first, later ball-bearings, and on such good-quality post-World War II models as the Austin J.40—see *pages 124-125* —double-roller bearings. Early cars generally have untreaded solid rubber tyres; later, treaded tyres of moulded rubber were fitted, with pneumatic tyres often to be found on the more expensive models.

BIBLIOGRAPHY

On the facing page, we have listed a number of books that we believe will be of assistance to both the novice and the established collector. Not all are still in print—some toy reference books have become collector's items in their own right!—but all should be available through libraries.

Above: *Colourful tinplate garages make attractive additions to a collection. (Left) "Shell" Filling Station by an unidentified West German maker; late 1950s. When the lever at the side of the lift is released, a spring mechanism raises the lift; a similar device on the pump causes the dial to revolve with a realistic sound.*

(Right) "Shell" Filling Station by Gama, West Germany; 1950s. A small clockwork car (not shown) is wound and placed in the garage. When the garage doors are opened, the car travels to the pump (guided by a clear plastic strip), "fills up", and then travels on out of the station to re-enter the garage at the rear.

Tin Toys 1945-1975 (London, 1978)
Michael Buhler

Discovering Toys and Toy Museums (Aylesbury, 1971)
Pauline Flick

An Illustrated History of Toys (London, 1965)
Karl Fritzsch & Manfred Bachman

The Price Guide to Metal Toys (Suffolk, 1980)
The Price Guide and Identification of Automobilia (Suffolk, 1982)
The All-Colour Directory of Metal Toys (London, 1984)
Gordon Gardiner & Alistair Morris

A History of British Dinky Toys 1934-1964 (Hemel Hempstead, 1966)
Veteran and Vintage Cars (London, 1970)
Racing and Record Cars (London, 1971)
Cecil Gibson

Catalogue of Model Cars of the World (Lausanne, Switzerland, 1967)
Jacques Greilsamer & Bertrand Azema

The Great Toys of George Carette (London, 1975)
Allen Levy

Cars for Kids (New York, 1983)
Edoardo Massucci

Toys (London, 1968)
Patrick Murray

The War Toys *kriegsspielzeuge:*
No 1, The Story of Hausser-Elastolin (London, 1979)
Reggie Polaine

The Art of the Tin Toy (London, 1976)
David Pressland

The Swapmeet & Toy Fair Catalogue of British Diecast Model Toys (Felixstowe, 1984)
John Ramsay (compiler)

The Golden Age of Toys (Lausanne, Switzerland, 1967)
Jac Remise & Jean Fondin

Dinky Toys & Modelled Miniatures (London, 1981)
Mike & Sue Richardson

History of French Dinky Toys 1933-1978 (Paris, 1978)
Jean-Michel Roulet

Model Cars and Road Vehicles (London, 1983)
Patrick Trench

Mechanical Tin Toys in Colour (Dorset, 1977)
Arno Weltens

The World of Model Cars (London, 1976)
Guy R. Williams

As well as being attractive and collectable items in their own right, the catalogues issued by toy makers are of great value as a source of information. They often list the sizes of the toys, their original price and their special features, and, of course, they are an invaluable aid to dating models accurately.

1 The cover of the catalogue issued around 1970 by Mercury, Italy, bears a chequered flag, indicating that it features the maker's series of racing cars. Examples of these are shown on *pages 88-89, 96-97* and *102-103*.

2 The cover of the catalogue issued in 1969 by Lesney Products Ltd, Great Britain, for the maker's "Matchbox" range of diecast vehicles: the 48-page colour publication was priced at 3d (1½p, 2c).

3 The cover of the catalogue issued in 1966 by Husky Models, Great Britain, to publicise the maker's range of diecast vehicles.

4 The cover of the catalogue issued in 1960 by Dinky Toys, France. This illustrates the range of Dinky Toys and Supertoys produced at Meccano's factory at Bobigny, near Paris, from the 1930s onward.

5 A spread from the colour catalogue issued in 1969 by Dinky Toys, France. It features saloon cars of the period; among them (bottom right) a model of the famous Volkswagen "Beetle", with opening bonnet, doors and rear engine compartment.

6 The cover of the catalogue issued in 1961 by Mini Cars (Anguplas), Spain, to publicise the maker's range of small plastic and diecast vehicles in 1:86 scale.

7 A spread from the catalogue issued in 1955-66 by Dinky Toys, France. Note how line drawings are used to emphasize various details of the models shown in the colour illustrations: the opening doors of the Ford Taunus; the opening bonnet of the Ferrari 250 GT Pininfarina Coupé; the stretcher and its occupant supplied with the Criterion Ambulance; the removable engine covers on the range of Grand Prix racing cars; and the opening boots of the Jaguar Mark X and the Triumph Spitfire.

8 A spread from the catalogue (Number 9) issued in 1973 by Dinky Toys, Great Britain. In this publication, smaller colour pictures are used to give information on the various special features of the models.

9 The dramatic cover of the catalogue issued in 1967 by Dinky Toys, France, showing sports racing cars.

10 This spread from the catalogue issued in 1980-81 by Solido, France, shows models in the maker's *Age d'Or* ("Golden Age") series of veteran cars. The coverage is international, with a Cord from the USA, a Renault and a Delahaye from France, and Rolls Royce cars representing Great Britain.

11 The cover of the English-language catalogue issued by Schuco (Schreyer and Company), West Germany, in 1949, not long after this long-established maker, founded in 1912, returned to production after World War II. Schuco has always been noted for the production of fine mechanical "novelty" vehicles, and the "Steerable Driving School Car" that features on the

cover of this catalogue would appear to fit well in that tradition. Note the serious, educational tone of the cover copy: although one may doubt the "permanent technical value" of "a model for instructing prospective motorists", there is no doubt that the toy itself is now even more avidly sought by collectors than this quite rare catalogue.

12 A spread from the catalogue issued in 1963 by Dinky Toys, France. This is a most attractive publication, both in the colour artwork of the models on the right-hand page and in the way those on the left are set against a photographic autoroute or motorway background.

13 This fold-out brochure was issued in 1952 by Tri-ang (Lines Brothers Ltd), Great Britain, to publicise its "Minic" range of vehicles and

accessories. These brochures were packed into the boxes in which the toys were sold. Clockwork-driven, tinplate Minic vehicles first appeared in the mid-1930s, and by the time production ended in the 1950s there were more than 70 models in the much-collected range.

14 The cover of the catalogue issued in 1976 by Solido, France. It shows a cross-section from the maker's range: modern and veteran cars, racing cars, and commercial and military vehicles and tanks.

15 The cover of the catalogue issued in 1962 by Corgi Toys, Great Britain; a 32-page booklet then priced at 3d (1½p, 2c). The artwork features a Jaguar Mk 10, a model of which (No 238, available until 1967) was issued by the maker in this year.

16 A spread from the French-language

catalogue issued in 1966 by Corgi Toys, Great Britain. It features three Gift Sets from the maker's range of racing, rally and speed cars, including (right) the two versions of the "All Winners Set" produced in 1966 only for export to France. Set No 45 consists of the James Bond DB5 Aston Martin (maker's reference number 261), Chevrolet Stingray (MRN 310), Marcos Volvo 1800 GT (MRN 324), Ford Mustang (MRN 325) and Ferrari Berlinetta 250 Le Mans (MRN 314). In Set No 46, the Jaguar "E" Type (MRN 312) replaces the Aston Martin. Note that the box shows the maker's name as "Playcraft Toys Ltd", the Swansea-based company (eventually to merge with the Mettoy Company) with which the trademark "Corgi", the

name of the best-known Welsh breed of dog, originated.

17 A spread from the catalogue issued in 1973 by Politoys (Polistil), Italy, to publicise its range of diecast cars. Note the graphic scale used to give specifications of the models' prototypes: a horse for horsepower; a speedometer for maximum speed (in kilometres per hour); a piston for the number of cylinders; and a cube for cubic capacity!

18 The cover of the catalogue issued in 1970 by Politoys (Polistil), Italy. Politoys' earlier models were of military vehicles and sports and racing cars in plastic, made to a scale of 1:41, and were produced from 1960 onward. In 1965, the company put into production its "500 Series" of cars in cast metal, most made in a scale of 1:43.

On this spread we show a selection of the boxes in which tinplate cars of the 1950s-60s were marketed. This period marked the last age of the mass-produced tinplate toy, which was killed off by the advent of plastic construction methods in the 1960s and, in the early 1970s, by legislation introduced in almost all countries to regulate the thickness of the metal that could be used. No doubt safety regulations were justified, since some cheaper, less well-finished toys of light-weight tinplate may be found to have razor-sharp edges, but one sometimes wonders how several generations of children survived virtually intact without the protection of paternalistic governments! We have heard dealers complain

that the collector's insistence on the provision of the original box is, in part at least, no more than a bargaining ploy to reduce the price of a non-boxed item. The dealer may argue that the intrinsic worth lies in the toy itself, and that the box is of no particular value. Nevertheless, it cannot be denied that the original packaging —often attractive in itself; frequently bearing detailed operating instructions; and sometimes carrying trademarks and slogans that do not appear on the toy itself—is a most desirable feature for the collector. Because packaging is fragile, perishable and ephemeral, it seems likely that the value of a boxed toy will increase significantly, as compared to an un-boxed item, as the years go by.

1 Box for Cadillac Gear Shift Car made by Bandai, Tokyo, Japan, in c1965; the toy itself is shown at (1), *pages 42-43*. Note the maker's serial number 4102 on the front (top left), and the illustrated operating instructions on the side of the box uppermost in the photograph. See also (2).
2 Box for Ferrari Gear Shift Car, maker's serial number 4183, made by Bandai in c1965; like the similar model shown at (1), this is a battery-powered toy. It is fully described at (5), pages 84-85. The illustrated operating instructions on the inside of the lid are clearly seen in this photograph; note also the Japanese maker's quaintly formal exhortation to the potential child customer: "Ask your Mama and Papa for

Bandai's battery operated toy!"
3 Box for Chrysler Imperial Convertible, Number 748 in Bandai's "Model Auto Series" (note serial number on box front, top left), dating from c1957-58. The toy itself, seen here on its box, is fully described at (5), *pages 42-43*.
4 "Hot Rod" Car by T.N. (Nomura Toys Limited), Tokyo, Japan, dating from c1957, shown here with its box on which the various action features of this colourful toy are listed and illustrated. A different view of the car is shown at (10), *pages 44-45*. Powered by two 1·5-volt batteries housed in a trap in the base, with an on/off switch (visible in this photograph) on its lower left side, the car pursues an eccentric course governed by twin driving-wheels

mounted on a turntable in the base, just behind the front wheels. A single spring-loaded wheel on a pivot is mounted towards the rear of the base; this is jointed to the head of the pressed-tin driver, causing it to turn in the direction taken by the car. When the car moves, the red and green lights atop the engine and the clear plastic cylinders at the sides of the bonnet light up. Pressed-tin headlights are fitted and bright metal details include the radiator, rear bumper (with a cut-out metal number plate, "H 12", above it), and windscreen frame; printed details include the exposed engine, exhaust manifolds, and the legends "Dream Boat" (left), "Hot Rod" (boot), and "Rock n' Roll" (*sic*) (right). It

has rubber wheels with bright metal discs. This has now become a rare toy: only a few examples are known to exist in Great Britain. Length: 7·375in (18·73cm).
5 Box for *Silberpfeil* (Silver Arrow) Racing Car by JNF, West Germany, dating from c1957-58; the toy itself, shown here in front of its box, is fully described at (7), *pages 84-85*. On the side of the box uppermost in the photograph is a universally-intelligible indication that the model features operating steering.
6 Box for Remote-Control Car made by Arnold, West Germany, in c1954. This toy was made in various colours and in two forms: as a Convertible—shown thus at (1), *pages 44-45*—and as a Saloon, as illustrated on the box, In either

form, it is now quite scarce.
7 Box for New Sedan by T.N. (Nomura Toys), Japan, dating from c1958. The toy itself, shown here on top of its box, is fully described at (1), *pages 40-41*.
8 Box for Racing Car (modelled on a Mercedes Type 196 racing car) made by JNF, West Germany; a version of this toy, in red finish, is shown and described at (4), *pages 84-85*. This toy appeared in c1957-58 in red or silver finish and in three different versions: friction-driven; battery-powered in multi-action form; and battery-powered with remote-control steering. It provides an interesting example of a manufacturer obtaining "added mileage" from the same basic pressing by issuing various modifications. In this

connection, note also that (5) and (8) are models of the same car, the Mercedes Type 196; (5) being a sports racing version.
9 Box for Plymouth Sedan by Ichiko, Japan, dating from c1958; the toy itself, which is now quite a scarce item, is described at (6), *pages 42-43*. The box is fairly typical of the packaging used by Japanese makers for their standard items of the period, featuring an attractive picture of the car (apparently passing Mount Fuji, on the lid overlap!); a brief statement of any special features—"Friction with Siren" on this model; the maker's trademark and the legend "Made in Japan"; and, in this case, the words "Pat. Pend." (Patent(s) Pending) at left on lid.

1 Ferrari 250LM by Mercury, Italy; a boxed diecast model dating from 1964. Note that the side of the box has a circular cutout so that the colour of the model can be checked without opening it, and that the artwork incorporates detail of a major feature—in this case a removeable bonnet.

2 Porsche Carrera 6 by Mercury, Italy, dating from 1967. As at (1), the box has a cutout circle and the artwork shows the opening gull-wing doors of the model.

3 Ferrari by Märklin, West Germany; this model, dating from c1965, is secured to a stiff card base and protected by a canopy of clear plastic.

4 Volkswagen 1500, by Tekno, Denmark; this model, dating from c1970, is seen in front of its rather unimaginative box.

5 Ferrari Daytona by Solido, France; this racing sports car, dating from c1970, is clearly visible to the prospective buyer in its window box, which also carries a French-language slogan claiming that Solido's cars are "always the best models".

6 Ford Mustang 2+2 Bertone by Politoys, Italy. The packaging of this model, dating from c1970, is similar to that of (3), but in this case the car is secured to a plastic base.

7 Alfa Romeo Duetta Spyder by Mebetoys, Italy. The window box in which this model, dating from 1967, is marketed bears the maker's serial number, "A18", along with information on the scale of the model, 1:43.

8 Matra 670 by Solido, France. This well-detailed racing car, dating from 1972, is packaged in a window box a little stouter than that of the Solido model at (5). The box gives some detail of the history of the car it contains, with the legend "Le Mans 72".

9 B.M.W. by Schuco, West Germany, dating from c1978. A foam rubber pad wedged between the car's roof and the hard plastic top of the display box protects the model. A stick-on label on the plastic base gives the maker's name, the model's scale (1:43), and details of its construction.

10-11 Two examples of boxes for Solido's series of racing cars ("Collection bolide"), made in the 1960s. Both boxes—for the Chaparral 2D (10) and Fiat Abarth (11); the latter model shown in front of its box—feature artwork of the contents and a helmeted-head series trademark. Visible on the side of the box at (10) is a French-language slogan: "The Monsters of Speed"! Note the cutaway circle at (11).

12 Cisitalia Model 202. The Italian-made model of Pininfarina-styled saloon, dating from c1960, shown here in front of its box, is Number 10 in a series marketed by a motor museum at Turin.

13 Alfa Romeo Giulia by Mercury, Italy. Dating from c1965, this rally car is packaged in an extremely robust plastic display pack, with Mercury's trademark embossed on the plastic top. The pack also contains a small figure "introducing" the model.

14 Racing Car by Gama, West Germany; the simple window box contains a small diecast model in the maker's "Mini" range.

15-17 Three examples of the packaging used at different periods for the models in the Spot On range made by Tri-ang (Lines Brothers Ltd), Great Britain, between 1959 and 1966. At (15): the first design characterised by the "dividers" (note the scale 1:42, the scale of all Spot On models, printed between the dividers' arms); a coloured picture of the real car was packed in all boxes of this early period. At (16): the final design, a window box; in this case containing the Hillman Minx, Number 287, issued in 1965. At (17): the second design, an all-card box (with the dividers

in much reduced size, just below the maker's name); in this case containing the Humber Super Snipe Estate Car, Number 183, issued in 1963. Note the promotional scheme announced on the side of the box: the sender of ten empty boxes would receive a free model (which presumably explains why so many surviving Spot On models are without their boxes!).

18 Lincoln Continental by Tekno, Denmark; another of this maker's rather dull boxes, for a model dating from around 1970.

19 Opel Rekord by Dinky Toys, France; Number 542, dating from 1964. As comparison with (20) and (21) shows, apart from the French-language inscriptions, including "Made in France", on the familiar yellow boxes, the

packaging of French Dinky Toys was near-identical to that of their British-made equivalents.

20 M.G.B. by Dinky Toys, Great Britain; Number 113, available 1963-68. The box features a chequered flag motif, drawing attention to Dinky's "1st sports car with opening doors", and a description of "fingertip steering".

21 A.C. Aceca Coupé by Dinky Toys, Great Britain; Number 167, available 1958-63.

22 Aston Martin DB3 Sport by Dinky Toys, France; Number 504, dating from around 1960.

23 Renault Frègate by CIJ (Compagnie Industrielle du Jouet), France; the simple model, dating from 1953, is shown here in front of its box.

24 Renault Dauphinoise by CIJ,

France; another simple model, here shown on top of its box.

25 Ford Capri Rally Car by Dinky Toys, Great Britain; Number 213, available 1971-74. By this time Dinky had adopted a plastic-topped display rack, with a card bottom simulating a highway.

26 DKW Junior by Tekno, Denmark, dating from 1962. The packaging has been brightened up a little to announce "fingertip steering".

27 Peugeot 504 by Polistil, France, dating from the 1970s.

28 Chevrolet Sport (Corvette Stingray) by Pilen, Spain; dating from around 1980.

29 Alfa Romeo Rally Car by Mercury, Italy; in contrast to the simple boxes at (1) and (2), this later model is housed in a tough plastic "Autobox".

37

All the cars shown on this spread are from the collection of Ron McCrindell, Sidmouth, Devon.

1 Limousine by Tipp and Company, Nuremburg, Germany; dating from around 1928. This most attractively lithographed tinplate toy, with lithographed chauffeur and pressed-tin wheels and "Dunlop Cord" tyres, is clockwork-driven. This is one of Tipp's range of cheaper cars, with non-opening doors, sold in Great Britain in the late 1920s at 1s 9d (8½p, 10c). For an extra 9d (3½p, 4c), the identical car could be purchased with electric headlights: flat, white-backed bulbs in a tin holder were connected to a battery clipped beneath the car. The aperture intended to accommodate the on/off lever for

these lights is visible on the running-board, along with the slots on the side of the bonnet to take the light-holders. Tipp's cars have become increasingly popular—especially as cars by Bing and Carette move ever further beyond the financial reach of many collectors—and the one shown, in mint condition, is a scarce and desirable item. Length: 9.84in (24.99cm).

2 Rear-Entrance Tonneau Car by an unidentified European maker; dating from around 1907. It bears on the front, below the windscreen, the trademark "R & Co B", surmounted by a crown and followed by the number "205" (which also appears on the bonnet). This early lithographed car, with chauffeur, is of extremely fragile construction:

the tinplate is wafer-thin, and it is powered by the kind of simple coiled-spring mechanism then favoured by makers of cheap, mass-produced toys. The roof of this example is a replacement. Length: 7.87in (19.99cm).

3 Open Tourer by Brimtoy, Great Britain; dating from around 1919. The maker's familiar "Nelson's Column" trademark, with the words "Brimtoy Brand, British Made", is on the underside—but it is most instructive to compare this car with the Bing toy shown at (5), since there is a strong possibility that this example, also, was made by Bing in Nuremburg. Its clockwork mechanism is certainly by Bing, and the metal pressings are identical in both cars, although the finish and quality of (5) are superior.

Only the wheels are of a type not found on Bing cars. Limited. Length: 10.5in (26.67mm).

4 Saloon Car by Bing, Nuremburg, Germany; dating from 1932. This lithographed tinplate toy, clockwork-driven (note fixed key), is rather uninspired in comparison to Bing's earlier products: it is an example of Bing's very last production run of toy cars, and a rather sad reminder of the great company's decline. It is, nevertheless, a desirable collector's item. Length: 9in (22.86cm).

5 Open Tourer by Bing; dating from around 1913. The similarities between this car and (3) have already been noted: a single glance reveals that this is a much superior item, of heavier construction and with dark blue livery that contrasts

most pleasantly with the brightly-lithographed seats. Other refinements include a glass windscreen and an operating hand-brake. Note also the brackets for nickel-plated side-lights, unfortunately missing from this example, as is the tinplate chauffeur originally fitted. Rare. Length: 12·5in (31·7cm).

6 Taxi by H. Fischer & Co, Nuremburg, Germany; dating from c1910. This most attractively lithographed representation of a Paris taxi, with opening doors, pressed-tin driver and a taxi-meter, is one of a large range of cars only recently attributed to Fischer, a prolific producer of tinplate trains and cars from c1908 until the 1930s. It is clockwork-driven, with a fixed key. Limited. Length: 8·66in (21·99cm).

7 Open Tourer by Karl Bub, Nuremburg, Germany; dating from 1927. A pleasantly solid car of lithographed tinplate, complete with chauffeur (apparently dozing!), this is clockwork-driven, with a fixed key just in front of the rear wheel. This toy was catalogued by Bub in 1927 in no fewer than six sizes, ranging from 5·9in (150mm), to the largest, as shown here, at 13in (33·02cm).

8 Roadster by an unidentified US maker; dating from around 1915. Constructed of tinplate and painted yellow, this sporty little car is most pleasantly evocative of its era. It has a realistic drive: the starting-handle protruding from the front is cranked to wind a coiled-spring mechanism. This particular example lacks its driver

and the spare wheel that would originally have been mounted on the boot (note hole). Scarce. Length: 9·055in (22·99cm).

9 "Penny Toys" Limousine by J. Ph. Meier/Kohnstam, Germany; dating from c1927. This little car in lithographed tinplate is a good late example of a "penny toy"— so-called because toys of this type were sold for 1d (0.42p, 0.5c), or its equivalent, when they were first made in the 1890s. Most originated in and around Nuremburg, where one of the best-known makers was J. Ph. Meier. The firm was later take over by Moses Kohnstam, who continued to market its products throughout the 1920s. Limited. Length: 3·937in (9·99cm).

10 Taxi; c1928; lithographed tinplate with a coiled-spring mechanism.

The taxi-flag, "Libre", suggests that it was intended for the French market—but since it bears the rear number plate "M.3.423", while the "penny toy" at (9) has the number "M.3.523", we may assume that both are by the same maker, and that this taxi is probably one of the few larger toys by Meier/Kohnstam. Rare. Length: 5·51in (13·9cm).

11 Open Tourer by Bing; dating from c1928. A fairly late item— see also (4)—but nevertheless a very attractive tinplate car, lithographed in a lovely shade of green which is nicely complemented by the striped seats, orange wheels and blue-uniformed chauffeur. It is fitted with the fixed-key clockwork mechanism standard on Bing's smaller cars of the period. Scarce. Length: 8·66in (21·9cm).

1 New Sedan by T.N. (Nomura Toys Limited), Tokyo, Japan, dating from c1958; it bears the maker's trademark and the words "Made in Japan" on the rear parcel shelf. This large and impressive toy is well-detailed, with a bright metal radiator and front and rear bumpers (incorporating pressed and printed head- and rearlights), mascot, front and rear windscreen frames (with clear plastic screens), and side trim strips enclosing a yellow printed area. The pressed-tin interior is similarly well-detailed, including a steering column and wheel. A rear-mounted number plate reads: "M-1127". The wheels are rubber, with metal discs bearing printed details of spokes and whitewalls. The toy is friction-driven, on the rear wheels.
Length: 11·25in (28·575cm).

2 Mercedes-Benz 220S by SSS International, Japan, c1958; it bears the words "Made in Japan" on the rear parcel shelf. Bright metal details include the radiator (the Mercedes star above it is plastic), headlights, front and rear bumpers, and front and rear windscreen frames (with a clear plastic front screen). It has a pressed and printed interior, with front and rear seats and a plastic steering wheel. A number plate, "220S", is fitted at the rear. The rubber wheels, with friction drive on the front pair, have metal hubcaps and whitewalls.
Length: 7·5in (19·05cm).

3 Station Wagon by an unidentified West German maker, c1956. The body pressing incorporates louvres in the front wings and an opening tailgate with a cast metal handle. The mascot is also cast metal, and as well as the usual brightwork details it has pressed-tin rear-lights applied by tab-and-slot. Rubber whitewall tyres are fitted to the metal wheels, the front pair friction-driven.
Length: 11·125in (28·257cm).

4 Station Wagon by "KKK", Japan, 1950s; the name "Country Squire" is printed across the front doors on either side and the maker's trademark and "Made in Japan" appear on the rear parcel shelf. Printed details on the body include simulated wooden side-panels; bright metal details include a roof rack. The rubber wheels have metal discs with printed spokes and whitewalls. Friction powers the front wheels. Length: 8·75in (22·225cm).

5 Sedan-Convertible by an unidentified maker, c1960-61. The words "Made in China" are printed on the rear parcel shelf. This is an attractive and pleasingly-detailed toy, with bright metal details that include trim strips. Number plates at front and rear read "MF 748". When the green lever to the left of the rear seats is turned, the boot opens and a tinplate hardtop swings up and over, the boot closing again as it snaps into place. The plastic wheels, with printed spokes and whitewalls, are fitted with rubber tyres; friction drives the front pair. Length: 9in (22·86cm).

6 Saloon Car by an unidentified Japanese maker, c1958; "Made in Japan" is printed on the boot, below a number plate "FD 6941".

It has printed details on bright
metal at front and rear and a simple
printed interior. The rubber wheels
(the rear pair friction-driven)
are fitted with metal discs.
Length: 5·75in (14·605cm).

7 Cadillac Sedan by an unidentified
Japanese maker, c1958; a Red
Indian Head trademark and "Made
in Japan" are printed below the
legend "Cadillac" on the left rear
wing. This simple toy in lightweight
tinplate has basic printed details
inside and out and is fitted with
rubber wheels and metal discs.
Friction drives the rear wheels.
Length: 4·75in (12·065cm).

8 "Gama 300" Saloon Car by Gama,
West Germany, c1956-57; note the
enamelled "Gama" badge above the
bright metal radiator and the legend
"Gama 300" in applied bright metal

letters along the front wings.
This good-quality toy features much
bright metal detail and a well-
printed pressed-tin interior, with
a plastic steering wheel (left-hand
drive). The metal wheels have rubber
tyres with inset plastic whitewalls. Friction drives the rear
wheels: the front wheels can be
manually turned for varied courses.
Length: 12·25in (31·115cm).

9-10 Convertible (9) and Hardtop
(10) by an unidentified Japanese
maker, c1958. These have the same
basic body pressing. Both have
"Fairlane 500" printed on both
sides of the rear wings: on the
Hardtop, "Japan" is printed below
this on the right side. The bright
metal details are fairly crude.
Transmission and suspension
details are printed on the bases.

Both cars have rubber wheels,
the front pair friction-driven, with
metal discs. Length: (each car):
6·25in (15·87cm).

11 Sedan by an unidentified
Japanese maker, c1958; the
word "Japan" is stamped on the
base. With little detail other
than the basic bright metal at
front and rear, this car has rubber
wheels, the rear pair friction-
driven, fitted with metal discs.
Length: 5in (12·7cm).

12 Limousine Car by Taguchi, Japan,
c1958. It bears a transfer
"Limousine" on both sides and tin
plates printed with same legend are
applied to the bright metal roof
rack. A large applied plate at
the rear is printed "Drive Carefully/
Airport". The flywheel for the
rear-wheel friction-drive is just

visible in the undetailed interior.
The wheels are rubber with metal
discs. Length: 5·375in (13·65cm).

13 New World Car by an unidentified
Japanese maker c1958; "Made in
Japan" is stamped on the base.
This simple tinplate toy lacks any
interior detail; it has the usual
bright metal exterior detail, including
discs on the rubber wheels.
Length: 5·25in (13·335cm).

14 Convertible by an unidentified
Japanese maker, c1958; the rear
number plate reads "Japan/M-372".
A brightly-printed friction-drive
(rear wheels) toy in lightweight
tinplate, this has tabbed-and-
slotted front and rear bumpers,
printed details of radiator,
mascot and interior, and rubber
wheels fitted with metal discs.
Length: 4in (10·16cm).

1 Cadillac Gear Shift Car by Bandai, Tokyo, Japan, made in c1965. This fine battery-driven toy has a tinplate body with a bright metal radiator grille and mascot and plated bumpers and door handles. The pressed-tin interior has printed upholstery detail; the windscreen, in a bright metal frame, is celluloid. Powered by two 1·5-volt batteries housed in a trap in the underside, it features operating steering (left-hand drive; like all the other representations of American cars on this spread), a working horn, and an "engine noise" mechanism. Its most notable features, however, are its working gear-levers, one giving high and low speeds and neutral gear, and the other giving forward, reverse and stop. It has well-modelled

plastic wheels fitted with rubber tyres. Length: 11·375in (28·89cm).
2 Chevrolet Convertible by Bandai, Japan; this is Number 710, dating from around 1960, in the maker's "Model Auto Series", which was marketed in boxes bearing the slogan "Over one hundred models. Start your collection now". See (5), (7), (8), (10) and (11) on this spread for other cars in the same series. Well-detailed, this friction-driven car has a bright metal radiator grille and front and rear bumpers, a tinted plastic windscreen framed in bright metal, and a pressed-tin interior with printed two-tone upholstery and a pressed-tin three-spoked steering wheel (left-hand drive). The pressed-tin wheels are painted with details of spokes, whitewalls and the

Chevrolet crest, and rubber tyres are fitted. The tinplate base bears printed details of transmission, exhaust system and suspension. Length: 6·25in (15·875cm).
3 New Ford Sedan by "H", Japan, c1957; the words "Made in Japan" are printed on the dashboard. This simple friction-drive car, with bright metal details and a printed interior, has rubber wheels fitted with bright metal discs. Length: 7·75in (19·685cm).
4 New Edsel by Haji (Mansei Toy Company), Japan, c1959. A well-detailed representation of Ford's ill-fated 1950's car (identified in bright metal letters on the rear wings), featuring the usual bright metal details and a printed interior with a pressed-tin steering wheel. A number plate at the rear

reads "84-A8259"; the maker's trademark is printed on the rear side of the front seats. The rubber wheels are fitted with metal whitewalls and hubcaps. Friction drives the front wheels. Length: 10·875in (27·62cm).
5 Chrysler Imperial Convertible; Number 748, dating from c1957-58, in Bandai's "Model Auto Series". All details of construction are as (2). On this toy note particularly the pressing for the boot-mounted spare wheel, with its bright metal disc, and the maker's applied paper label—"Model Auto Series/ Imperial Group"—on the rear parcel shelf. Length: 8·5in (21·59cm).
6 Plymouth Sedan by Ichiko, Japan, c1958. An attractive toy, with the usual brightwork details, including side trim strips and gilt

metal sidelights, this has a nicely-printed interior. It has pressed-tin wheels with rubber tyres and is friction-driven, with a mechanism producing a "siren" sound. Length: 6·375in (16·19cm).

7 Chevrolet Station Wagon; Number 716 in Bandai's "Model Auto Series". All details of construction are as (2). The maker's applied paper label on the bonnet reads: "Model Auto Series/Chevrolet Group". Note that the tinted plastic windscreen is not matched by a rear window. Length: 8·375in (21·27cm).

8 Buick Convertible; Number 723, dating from c1959, in Bandai's "Model Auto Series". All details of construction are as (2). Length: 6·125in (15·56cm).

9 New Desoto by Taiyo (Taiyo Kogyo Company), Tokyo, Japan,

c1957; it is marked "Made in Japan" on the rear parcel shelf. An applied tin trim strip in blue supplements the usual brightwork detail on this friction-drive car, which has lightly-tinted plastic front and rear screens. The wheels and tyres are rubber, with pressed-tin discs. Length: 7·875in (20cm).

10 Ford Thunderbird; Number 716, dating from c1957, in Bandai's "Model Auto Series", and heralded on the box as "America's Most Individual Car". All details of construction are as (2). Length: 8·5in (21·5cm).

11 Pontiac Convertible; Number 711, dating from c1957, in Bandai's "Model Auto Series". All details of construction are as (2). The maker's applied paper label on the automobile's boot reads: "Model

Auto Series/Pontiac Group". Length: 6·125in (15·56cm).

12 "Fairlane 500" Sedan by an unidentified Japanese maker, dating from c1957: the legend "Made in Japan" is stamped below the words "Fairlane 500" on the side of the model facing away from the camera in this photograph. For such a small toy, it is well-detailed, with a nicely-printed interior. It has rubber wheels (the front pair friction-driven) with metal discs. Length: 4·25in (10·795cm).

13-15 "Three-Style Car" by "MT" (Modern Toys; K.K. Masutoku Toy Factory), Tokyo, Japan, dating from c1958. Produced by one of the more senior Japanese makers, in operation since 1924, this set features the same body pressing in three different finishes: a Yellow

Taxi, printed "Yellow Cab" on boot top (13), a Desoto Sedan (14), and a Checker Taxi (15). Note the bright metal bumpers on these fairly basic tinplate, friction-drive cars, and the figures of drivers and passengers printed on the upper bodies. Applied metal plates at the rear—just visible on (13) and (15) in this photograph—bear road safety slogans. The rubber wheels are fitted with bright metal discs. These little cars are typical of the cheaper toys of the period: they were made of very light tinplate, permitting the kind of lithography that would not be possible on the heavier-gauge metal required under modern safety regulations. Length (each car): 5·875in (14·92cm).

1 Remote-Control Convertible by Arnold, West Germany, made in c1954. This is a fairly simple tinplate toy, with pressed-tin seats printed in a tartan pattern and bright metal detail, including front and rear bumpers, radiator and mascot. The steering wheel (right-hand drive) and wraparound windscreen are plastic; the driver is a composition figure. It has plastic wheels with metal discs and rubber whitewall tyres; the name "Arnold" is stamped on the whitewalls, and the Arnold trademark and the words "Made in Western Germany" are also stamped on the bright metal base. The line transmitting power from the handset consists of an outer and an inner cable: the handle on the handset turns the outer cable,

which joins a sprocket in the car and acts through a crown-wheel and piston to give forward or reverse motion; the inner cable, activated by the plunger on the handset, steers the car right (pushed in) or left (pulled out). Length: 10in (25·4cm).

2 Mercedes-Benz Remote-Control Sedan by Arnold, West Germany, c1957. A simple but attractive toy: the body is a single pressing, tabbed-and-slotted to the base plate, and all the detail—the Mercedes star, the colourful driver (left-hand drive) and passenger, and the simulation of the "gull-wing" doors that featured on the real car—is printed. The wheels are rubber. It is remote-controlled by the same system as (1), and has the same maker's marks on the

base. Length: 11·75in (29·845cm).

3 Streamline Electric Sedan by an unidentified maker, c1961; a paper sticker on the base reads "Made in the People's Republic of China" in both English and Chinese. This American-styled car (left-hand drive), with pressed-tin fins rather clumsily tabbed on, has the usual bright metal detail—radiator, bumpers, windscreen frames, body trim, door handles and mascot—and has a pressed-tin interior with a plastic steering wheel. The head- and rear-lights are of coloured plastic and a rear-mounted number plate of gilt metal bears the number "10100". The wheels, whitewalls and hubcaps are metal, with rubber tyres. Battery-powered, with an on/off switch on the base, the car runs

a variable course determined by a single pivoted wheel mounted between its front wheels. Length: 9·5in (24·13cm).

4 Convertible by "KY", People's Republic of China, c1966: note maker's mark on hubcaps. It has bright metal front and rear trim, coloured plastic side- and rear-lights, and a plastic mascot above the radiator. The pressed-tin interior has simple printed upholstery detail and the driver, a rubber half-figure in Mao-style dress, sits behind a plastic steering wheel (left-hand drive). The wheels and whitewalls are plastic, with metal hubcaps and rubber tyres. A rear-mounted number plate reads: "ME-612". Batteries power the near-side wheel and the front wheels are spring-

loaded to steer in a circle. Length: 9·75in (24·765cm).

5 Jeep by Ites (Koh-I-Noor Hardtmuth), Czechoslovakia, 1950s. This is a robust tinplate toy of simple tab-and-slot construction, featuring a perspex windscreen that folds forward and a rear-mounted spare wheel. The wheels are plastic with rubber tyres. Clockwork (note the winding shaft in the bonnet) powers the front wheels of this left-hand drive car. Length: 7in (17·78cm).

6 M101 Aston-Martin Secret Ejector Car by an unidentified Japanese maker, 1960s. Inspired by the "James Bond" films (but not described as a "James Bond" car on its box), this ingenious toy features a remotely-operated "bullet-proof" shield at the rear,

realistically-sparking machine guns at the front, crash bumpers that extend and retract, and push-button ejection of the plastic passenger through a roof trap. Power is supplied by three 1·5-volt batteries in the handset, and a two-wheel swivel in the base gives a variable course. The radiator, bumpers, lights and tinted wind-screens are plastic; the rubber wheels have plastic discs printed with details of spokes and hubcaps. The words "Made in Japan" are stamped on the rear parcel shelf. Length: 11in (27·94cm).

7-9 Three Assorted Cars, marketed together as a boxed set with this title, by "K", Japan, 1950s-60s. These simple tinplate cars—a Convertible (7), Sedan (8) and Station Wagon (9)—are all of the

same basic construction, with rubber wheels fitted with metal discs, and are friction-powered (rear wheels). All bear the trade-mark "K" and the words "Made in Japan" on the left rear wing. A fairly scarce set. Length: (each car): 4·19in (10·64cm).

10 Hot Rod by T.N. (Nomura Toys), Japan, c1957. This colourful battery-powered toy is fully decribed at (4), *pages 34-35*, where it is shown with its original box. Length: 7·375in (18·73cm).

11 MGA Sports Roadster by Lincoln International, Hong Kong, 1960s. Note that the body pressing is the same as that of the MGA Hardtop at (12). It has the usual brightwork detail. The figure of the driver (right-hand drive) is rubber and the wheels, also rubber, have

metal discs. Two 1·5-volt batteries in the handset allow the car to be driven forward or in reverse, but it cannot be steered. Length: 7in (17·78cm).

12 MGA Hardtop Sports Saloon by Motorway Models; this utilizes the same body pressing as (11), with the addition of a black hardtop and pressed-tin door- and boot-handles, and is presumably a Hong Kong-made toy of the same period; its base is stamped "Empire Made". It is friction-powered (rear wheels). Length: 7in (17·78cm).

13 Jaguar XK150 by an unidentified maker—the base is stamped "Empire Made"—dating from the 1960s. With brightwork details, it has a basic pressed-tin interior and is friction-powered (rear wheels). Length: 6in (15·24cm).

1 Ambulance by Dinky Toys, Great Britain; Dinky Toys Reference Number (DT No) 30f. Shown here is the fourth version, dating from 1947-48, of a model first issued in August 1935. The identification points of the various versions are: (1935-38) red-and-grey body, moulded chassis, plain radiator and open side windows; (1938-40) black-and-grey body, moulded chassis, radiator with badge, open side windows; (1947-48), as seen, with cream body, black moulded chassis, no side windows. All versions have red crosses on the sides. Both the pre-World War II versions are rare; both post-War versions are quite common. Length: 3·898in (99mm).

2 Ambulance; DT No 24a. This is the original version of the model first issued in April 1934 and available in this form until 1938. It appeared in cream-and-red or grey-and-red and had a criss-cross chassis and a plain radiator. The second version, issued in 1938-40, was made in green-and-red or grey-and-red and had a radiator with a badge. Both versions are rare. Length: 4·016in (102mm).

3-5 Daimler; DT No 30c. This model was first issued in August 1935 and was made until 1940 in green, fawn, brown and light blue body finishes. It was reissued in 1946, remaining available until 1950, in green-and-black (3), cream-and-black (4), and brown-and-black (5), and possibly in other colours. The pre-War version has an open chassis; the post-War version may be found with an open chassis or a plain chassis. The pre-War version is rare; the post-War version is limited. Length: 3·858in (98mm).

6-8 Vauxhall; DT No 30d. Shown here are three examples, displaying colour variations, of the final version, dating from 1946-48, of a long-lived model. The first version, issued in 1935 and available until 1938, is identifiable by its brown open chassis and its wing-mounted spare wheel. The second version, made in 1937-38, has no spare wheel. The third version, made in 1938-40, has a radiator with a badge, and may be found with or without a spare wheel. The fourth version, as shown, is the only one made with a black (open or plain) chassis; it has no spare wheel. The three pre-War versions are rare; the post-War version is of limited availability. Length: 3·858in (98mm).

9 Chrysler "Airflow" Saloon by Dinky Toys, Great Britain. This model was announced as DT No 32 in January 1935, but by June 1935 it had appeared as DT No 30a. A one-piece casting with no chassis, it appeared in two versions. The first version, 1935-40, was made in blue or green. The second version, reissued in 1946 and available until 1948, was made in blue, cream or green. The pre-War version is rare; the post-War version is scarce. Length: 4·055in (103mm).

10-11 Austin 7 Saloon; DT No 35a. This model was first issued in 1936 and was available in grey only until 1940; these pre-War examples have white solid rubber wheels. It was reissued in 1946

and remained available until 1948;
post-War versions, like the two
shown here, have black solid rubber
wheels. Both versions are fairly
scarce. Length: 2·008in (51mm).

12-13 Austin 7 Tourer; DT No 35d.
First issued in 1938, this appeared
up to 1940 in several colours, with
a wire windscreen and white solid
rubber wheels. It was reissued in
1946-48, as shown, lacking the
windscreen and with black solid
rubber wheels. Both versions are
limited. Length: 1·969in (50mm).

14 Grand Sport (4-Seater) by Dinky
Toys, France; French Dinky Toys
Reference Number (FDT No) 24g,
dating from 1935-48. This is the
French-made version of the Sports
Tourer (4-Seater), second version,
issued by Dinky Toys, Great Britain,
in 1938-40. Note that the French

models shown at (14-17) have solid
wheels and tyres of post-1940 type.
Length: 3·858in (98mm).

15 Grand Sport Coupé; FDT No 24f:
the French-made version of the
Sportsman's Coupé (second
version) made in Britain in 1938-40.
Length: 3·937in (100mm).

16 Grand Sport (2-Seater); FDT No
24h: the French-made version of the
Sports Tourer (2-Seater), second
version, made in Britain in 1938-
40. Length: 3·858in (98mm).

17 Limousine; FDT No 24b: the
French-made version of the model
made with same name and
number in Britain in 1938-40
(second version). Length:
3·858in (98mm).

18-20 Rolls Royce by Dinky Toys,
Great Britain; DT No 30b. This
model was first issued in August

1935 and was made in various
colours, with an open chassis, until
1940. It was reissued, as shown, in
various colours, with black open
or plain chassis, in 1946-50. The
pre-War version is rare; the post-
War version is limited. Length:
3·976in (101mm).

21 Fiat (2-Seater) Saloon by Dinky
Toys, France; FDT No 35a. This
model, first issued in July 1939,
was marketed in France as the
Simca 5 (since the Fiat 500
"Topolino" was known by that
designation in France, where it was
manufactured under licence by
Simca) and in Britain as a Fiat,
DT No 35az. It has rubber wheels
and is a simple one-piece casting
with no base plate. Length:
2·323in (59mm).

22 Vogue Saloon; FDT No 24d: the

French version of the model made
in Britain under the same name and
number in 1938-40 (second
version). Note that this and (23)
are fitted with wheels and tyres
of pre-1940 type. Length:
4·016in (102mm).

23 Super Streamline Saloon; FDT
No 24e: the French version of the
model made in Britain under the
same name and reference number
in 1938-40 (second version).
Length: 3·819in (97mm).

24 Peugeot Car; FDT No 24k. First
issued in July 1939 and available
only until 1940, this model was
marketed in France as the Peugeot
402 and in Great Britain as the
Peugeot Car, DT No 24kz; see also
(21). Appearing only in red finish,
as shown, it has a tinplate front
bumper. Length: 3·74in (95mm).

47

Diecast Cars by Dinky Toys, Great Britain, 1938-1948

Inset: *(Right) A modern copy of the Limousine, DT No 24b; a "24 Series" model first issued in 1934 (although the absence of a wing-mounted spare wheel marks this example as a copy of the later version, issued in 1938). (Left) The "criss-cross" chassis, as seen in this modern copy of the "24 Series" Sportsman's Coupé, DT No 24f, was used only from 1934 to 1938.*

All the toy cars of the Dinky Toys "36 Series" are shown here. The range was announced in July 1938, when all six models of British "quality" cars of the time became available either separately or as a complete set, priced then at 5s 6d (27½p, 33c). Dinky based these models on the body castings of the "24 Series", first issued in 1934, but without the wing-mounted spare wheels that featured in the earlier series, and with the notable addition of "make" radiators in place of a universal type. As noted below, in the pre-War examples provision was made for fitting figures (tinplate in the closed cars; cast metal in the open models) of drivers and passengers. Not all pre-War versions of the series

were fitted with such figures, and examples in which they are present are now very highly valued by collectors of Dinky Toys.

1-2 Rover Saloon, Dinky Toys Reference Number (DT No) 36d. The cars shown here are post-World War II versions of the model made from 1938 to 1940 as the Rover Streamlined Saloon, under the same reference number. The post-War version, made from 1946 to 1948, was produced, as seen here, with a blue (1) or green (2) body on a black moulded chassis. The pre-War version was produced with a green or black body on a green chassis, or in two-tone red. Its moulded chassis was pierced to accommodate the tinplate figures of a driver and passenger (although

these figures were not always fitted); this feature was absent from the post-War version. Both versions were fitted with "make" radiators; note the Rover badge visible at (1). The pre-War version complete with figures is very rare—and neither the pre-War version without figures nor the post-War version shown here is common. Note that the lengths given for this car and others here are taken from post-War examples. Because of metal fatigue, pre-War cars may now prove to be as much as 0·275in (7mm) long than post-War examples. Length: 3·7in (94mm).
3-5 Bentley Two-Seater Sports Coupé, DT No 36b. This model first appeared in July 1938, when it was priced at 11d (4½p, 5c), and remained in production until 1940.

The examples shown here, however, are post-War versions, produced between 1946 and 1948. The pre-War version was made with a green and black or cream and black body (other colours may also have been used) and had a base plate pierced with slots to accommodate the tinplate figures of driver and passenger (not always fitted). This feature did not appear in the post-War models, which were made with green (5), grey, cream (3) or blue (4) bodies (again, other colours may have been used). Both versions had a moulded chassis. The rarest examples are those complete with driver and passenger; the pre-War version without figures may prove hard to find, but post-War versions are not uncommon. Length: 3·661in (93mm).

6 7 8 9 10 5 11 12 13 14 15

6-10 Armstrong-Siddeley
Limousine, DT No 36a. This model
was first issued in July 1938, at
the then standard price for "36
Series" models of 11d (4½p, 5c),
and remained in production until
1940. Like the other models in the
series, it was reissued under the
same reference number in 1946-48.
The pre-War version was produced
with a blue or brown and black
body; the post-War version, as
seen here, in green (6), maroon
(7), blue (8-9) or grey (10). Both
versions had a moulded chassis,
but in the pre-War model the base
plate was pierced with slots to
accommodate the tinplate figure
of driver and passenger (or
footman, since these were "quality"
cars!). As usual, models complete
with figures are the most valuable.

Length: 3·819in (97mm).

11-12 British Salmson (Four-Seater
Sports), DT No 36f. The pre-War
version, issued from July 1938 to
1940, was produced with a red and
brown or a two-tone green body;
the post-War version, as seen here,
produced in 1946-48, had a green
(11) or grey (12) body on a black
chassis. Both versions had a
moulded chassis and a solid
windscreen; in the pre-War model,
the front seat was pierced with a
hole to accommodate the peg-in
diecast figure of a driver. The
post-War version has no such hole
and has a cast-in steering wheel.
Again, the pre-War version with
driver is very rare, and all
versions of the four-seater
Salmson may prove hard to find.
Length: 3·779in (96mm).

13-15 British Salmson (Two-Seater
Sports), DT No 36e. The pre-War
version, made in 1938-40, appeared
in red and black, blue and black,
or with a grey body on a red
moulded chassis (other colours may
also be found); the post-War model,
as seen here, was made only in
red (13) or blue (14-15), on a
black moulded chassis, in 1946-48.
Some, but not all, pre-War versions
were made with a rubber spare
wheel on the right hand side; the
spare wheel was never fitted on
post-War models. The seat of the
pre-War model was pierced with a
hole for a peg-in diecast driver
and, as usual, the pre-War model
with driver is now rare and
valuable; even without the driver
it is hard to find. The solid
windscreen is common to all

versions, but only the post-War
model has a cast-in steering wheel.
Length: 3·661in (93mm).

16-18 Humber Vogue, DT No 36c.
The pre-War version, produced in
1938-40, was made in grey and
black, two-tone green, and probably
in other colours; the post-War
model, as shown, was made in
1946-48 in green and black, blue
and black (16), brown and black (17)
and grey and black (18). In the
pre-War version the moulded
chassis was slotted for the tinplate
figures of a driver and passenger;
as usual, this feature was absent
in the moulded chassis of the post-
War model. The model complete
with tinplate figures is rare and
valuable and no pre-War version
of this car is at all common.
Length: 3·819in (97mm).

Diecast Sports Cars by Dinky Toys, Great Britain, 1939-1960

Above: *A modern copy of the Triumph Dolomite Sports Coupé announced in 1939 as No 38e of Dinky's "38 Series". War halted production and this model was never issued: it was replaced in 1946 by the Armstrong-Siddeley shown at (1-2).*

1-2 Armstrong-Siddeley Coupé, Dinky Toys Reference Number (DT No) 38e. This model was introduced in December 1946, replacing the planned Triumph Dolomite (see *Inset*) in the "38 Series". It was Dinky's first model of a car of post-World War II manufacture, and remained in production until late 1949 or early 1950. It has a plastic windscreen and detachable rubber tyres; the black-painted tinplate base bears the maker's name and "Armstrong-Siddeley". This model may prove hard to find. Length: 3·78in (96mm).

3-4 Lagonda Sports Coupé, DT No 38c. This model was introduced in April 1946 and was deleted from the catalogue in 1950. It was made in grey with grey seats (3), in green with matt black seats (4),

and in maroon with black seats. The black-painted base plate bears the maker's name and "Lagonda". Again it has a plastic windscreen and detachable rubber tyres; the separately-cast steering wheel may be found in both solid and open forms. This is quite a scarce model. Length: 4·016in (102mm).

5-7 Sunbeam-Talbot Sports, DT No 38b. This model was announced in June 1939, along with five other "38 Series" sports cars: the Frazer-Nash B.M.W., No 38a, see (10-12); Lagonda, 38c (3-4); Alvis, 38d (8-9); Triumph Dolomite, 38e, (Inset); and Jaguar, 38f (13-15). Of these, only the Frazer-Nash B.M.W., Sunbeam-Talbot and Alvis were in production, probably only in small numbers, before World War II halted production in 1940. The

model shown here was reissued in 1946 and deleted in 1949. Both pre- and post-War versions were made in various colous, of which three variations are shown here, with matt-painted tonneau covers. The only major difference between pre- and post-War versions is that the former have unpainted tinplate base plates and the latter black-painted base plates; in both cases they bear the maker's name and "Sunbeam-Talbot". In post-War versions the steering wheel may be solid or open; both versions have a plastic windscreen, slotted into the base, and rubber tyres. Neither is common. Length: 3·622in (92mm).

8-9 Alvis Sports Tourer, DT No 38d. The production history of this "38 Series" sports car is the same as that of the Sunbeam-Talbot

Sports (5-7). Again, it was made in a number of colour schemes and had a plastic windscreen and detachable rubber tyres. Pre-War versions have a bare metal base plate, post-War versions a black-painted one, in both cases bearing the maker's name and "Alvis". In post-War models the steering wheel may be solid or open. As in the Lagonda (3-4), Sunbeam-Talbot (5-7) and Jaguar (13-15), the headlights are separately cast and are set into the front wings, while the steering wheels are also separate castings: both features are liable to be lost or damaged. All versions of the Alvis are fairly scarce. Length: 3·74in (95mm).

10-12 Frazer-Nash B.M.W. Sports Car, DT No 38a; production history as (5-7) and (8-9). Neither pre-

nor post-War versions are easy to find. Length: 3·228in (82mm).

13-15 Jaguar Sports Car, DT No 38f. This model of the famous "SS 100" was announced, as noted above, in June 1939, but it is probable that none was made before its "re-issue" in November 1946. It was deleted in 1949. Made in at least three colours, with the contrasting seats typical of the series, it had a black-painted base plate bearing the maker's name and "Jaguar". Note particularly the two small plastic windscreens. Like most models in the "38 Series", this is fairly scarce. Length: 3·15in (80mm).

16 Austin A90 Atlantic, DT No 106. This was originally issued in April 1951 as the Austin Atlantic Convertible, No 140a; it was re-

numbered in 1954 and remained in production until 1958. It was made in blue, as seen, black or pink, and is comparatively scarce. Length: 3·74in (95mm).

17 Sunbeam Alpine (Competition Finish), DT No 107. This was first issued in November 1955 and was deleted in 1959. It was made with a blue body with the racing number "26", as seen, and in pink with the number "34". Like (18-21), it was later issued in "touring finish" —see (22). It is quite scarce. Length: 3·70in (94mm).

18 M.G. Midget (Competition Finish), DT No 108. First issued in April 1955, this model of an M.G. TF was deleted in 1959. It was made with a white body numbered "28", as shown, or in red numbered "24"; see also (22). Again, quite a scarce

item. Length: 3·268in (83mm).

19 Austin Healey 100 (Competition Finish), DT No 109. First issued in June 1955 and deleted in 1959, this was produced in yellow numbered "21", as shown, or in cream numbered "23". It is quite scarce. Length: 3·346in (85mm).

20 Aston Martin DB3S (Competition Finish), DT No 110. Issued in March 1956, and made in green with the number "22", as shown, or in grey, this model differed from the others in the series in having no plastic windscreen. It was deleted in 1959. It is more easily found than the other sports cars shown on this spread. Length: 3·425in (87mm).

21 Triumph T.R.2 (Competition Finish), DT No 111. Introduced in February 1956, this model was made in pink with the number "29",

as shown, or in turquoise with the number "25". It was deleted in 1959. Again, it may prove hard to find. Length: 3·307in (84mm).

22 M.G. Midget (Touring Finish), DT No 102. First issued in August 1957, and made in green, as shown, or yellow, this was the touring version, with a driver in civilian clothes rather than racing overalls, and bearing no racing number, of the M.G Midget, No 108, see (18). The Sunbeam Alpine (17), Austin Healey 100 (19), Aston Martin DB3S (20), and Triumph T.R.2 (21) were issued in similar "touring versions" in 1957, numbered DT No 101, 103, 104 and 105 respectively. All were deleted in 1960. Like the version in competition finish, this MG in touring finish is fairly scarce. Length: 3·268in (83mm).

1-2 Packard Super 8 Touring Sedan Car, Dinky Toys Reference Number (DT No) 39a. This model was first announced in June-July 1939 as part of the "39 Series" set, along with the Oldsmobile Six Sedan Car (see 3-4); the Lincoln Zephyr Coupé (5-6); the Buick Viceroy Saloon Car (7-8); the Chrysler Royal Sedan (9-10); and the Studebaker State Commander Saloon Car (11-12). It is probable that these models were not, in fact, issued until 1940, and by 1941 all production had been ended by World War II. However, the set was re-issued, with the changes detailed below, in 1946 and remained available until 1949-50. All the cars in the set could, of course, be purchased as separate items. When first issued, priced at 10d

(4p, 5c) each pre-War, these constituted Dinky's first set of American cars and, another innovation, each had its name stamped on the base plate. The two versions of the Packard Super 8 shown here date from 1946-50, when the model was issued in brown (1) or green (2), with silver trim, with a black-painted base plate. The pre-War version, issued in brown or grey, with silver trim, had an unpainted tinplate base plate. Both versions had an open chassis and detachable rubber tyres (these two features being common to all the models in the series), a moulded spare wheel on the left wing, and separately-cast headlights. Neither version is particularly easy to find, the pre-War car being

considerably the rarer. Length: 4·21in (107mm).
3-4 Oldsmobile Six Sedan Car, DT No 39b; production history as (1-2). The post-War version was made in blue (3), grey (4), green or brown finish, with silver trim, and had a black-painted tinplate base plate. The pre-War version was issued in blue or green with silver trim and had an unpainted base plate. The pre-War version is scarce; post-War examples are quite scarce. Length: 3·937in (100mm).
5-6 Lincoln Zephyr Coupé, DT No 39c; production history as (1-2). The post-War version was available in brown (5) or grey (6) and had a black-painted tinplate base plate; the pre-War version was available in grey, brown or cream and had an unpainted base plate. Again, the

pre-War version is quite rare, and even the post-War version is hard to find. Length: 4·17in (106mm).
7-8 Buick Viceroy Saloon Car, DT No 39d; production history as (1-2), but note that production of this model may have ended in 1949. The pre-War version was issued in maroon (7) or grey (8) finish, with an unpainted base plate; the post-War version appeared in brown, green or maroon, with black-painted base plate. As in (1-2), both versions had a moulded spare wheel and separately-cast headlights. Current availability of this car is as (5-6). Length: 4·055in (103mm).
9-10 Chrysler Royal Sedan, DT No 39e; production history as (1-2), but again production may have ended in 1949. The pre-War version was made in blue, green (9), grey

Inset: *The unpainted, bare metal base plate distinguishes this model as a pre-War version of the Chrysler Royal Sedan; Number 39e of Dinky Toys' "39 Series".*

(10), or yellow finish, with an unpainted base plate; the post-War version appeared in blue, cream or grey, with a black-painted base plate. Current availability as (5-6). Length: 4·17in (106mm).

11-12 Studebaker State Commander Saloon Car, DT No 39f; production history as (1-2), but production may have ended in 1949. The pre-War version was made in green (11), dark grey or yellow, with unpainted base plate; the post-War version in green, blue (12), brown or grey, with black-painted base plate. Current availability as (5-6). Length: 4·055in (103mm).

13 Estate Car, DT No 27f. This model was first issued in February 1950, when it was priced at 2s 10d (14p, 17c) and was classified as one of Dinky's series of farm vehicles; it was renumbered 344 in 1954 and remained in production until 1956. It was issued only as shown here, with a fawn body and brown simulated-wood side panels. This car should not be too hard to find. Length: 4·134in (105mm).

14-15 Ford Fordor Sedan, DT No 139a. This model was first issued in August 1949, priced at 2s 6d (12½p, 15c), when it may have been intended as the first of a new series—the "139 Series" of US cars to follow the "39 Series" that was then beginning to go out of production; see also (16-17). It was renumbered 170 in 1954 and remained in production until 1959. The same casting was used for the Ford Fordor US Army Staff Car, in matt green finish with a white star on the bonnet, which was made in 1957-58 for the US market (some examples appear to have been sold in the UK). It appeared in 1949-54 with a red or brown body; in 1954-56 with a red, green (14) or yellow (15) body; and in 1956-59 in two-tone finish, either cream-and-red or pink-and-blue. The US Army Staff Car version is rare in the UK; the brown-finished 1949-54 version may be a little harder to find than the others, while the two-tone versions are the most common. Length: 4·016in (102mm).

16-17 Hudson Commodore Sedan, DT No 139b. This model was first issued in July 1950, was renumbered 171 in 1954 and was deleted in 1958. It was issued in 1950-56 in two-tone finish, either maroon-and-fawn (16) or fawn-and-blue (17), and in 1956-58 in either red-and-blue or blue-and-grey. The later versions may prove harder to find. Length: 4·37 (111mm).

18-19 Studebaker Land Cruiser, DT No 172. This model was issued in April 1954, just one month after Dinky Toys abandoned its former practice of giving each model a letter as well as a number. Priced initially at 2s 8d (13p, 16c), it was issued until July 1956 in green or blue (18) finish, and from then until 1958, when it went out of production, in two-tone finish, either maroon-and-cream or fawn-and-brown (19). On the earlier versions, the tinplate base is stamped with the maker's name and "Studebaker"; later versions also bear the number "172". In neither case should it be too hard to find. Length: 4·21in (107mm).

Inset (above): *Variations in the chassis of the Standard Vanguard Saloon, DT No 40e (renumbered 153 in 1955); see also notes at (11-14) below. In both cases the chassis of the first version (1948-50) is shown, with open rear wheel arches and the information on the tinplate base plate stamped in small letters—but note the variation in the method used to secure the rear axle of the model.*

1-4 Riley Saloon, Dinky Toys Reference Number (DT No) 40a. This was the first model in the "40 Series" of British cars (the "39 Series" consisted of models of American cars; see *pages 52-53*) and was issued in July 1947. It was renumbered 158 in 1955 and remained in production until 1960.

5-6 Triumph 1800 Saloon, DT No 40b. The second model in the "40 Series", this was first issued in July 1948. The first version, made only in 1948-49 and in fawn, blue or grey finish, had its rear axle

Between 1947 and 1955 the model was issued in grey (1), blue (2), cream (3) or green (4) finish, with a tinplate base plate stamped with the maker's name and model designation in small capital letters. Between March 1954 and 1960 (there was some overlap between the versions, as is the case with other models described here) it appeared in blue or cream, with the letters on the base plate in large letters. See also *Inset* (top right). Neither version should be too hard to find. Length: 3·66in (93mm).

held in place by pillars on either side and had a tinplate base plate stamped with the maker's name and the number "40B". The second version, made between 1949 and 1955, appeared in the same colours but had its rear axle held in place by the base plate, which was stamped only with the maker's name. In 1955 the model was renumbered 151, and thereafter appeared in blue (5) or brown (6) until 1960, with a base plate stamped with the maker's name and "Triumph". The first and second versions are more highly valued. Length: 3·583in (91mm).

7-10 Austin Devon Saloon, DT No 40d. The third car in the "40 Series" (the number 40c was not used), this appeared in January 1949. It was made in blue (7),

green (8) or maroon (9) finish, with a base plate stamped with the maker's name and "40D", until 1955, when it was renumbered 152. In 1954-56 it appeared in maroon or blue, with the base plate stamped with the maker's name and "Austin Devon". From August 1956 until production ended in 1960, it was made in two-tone finishes, either blue-and-yellow (10) or grey-and-cerise, the base plate being the same. No version is particularly rare. Length: 3·346in (85mm).

11-14 Standard Vanguard Saloon, DT No 40e. The fourth car in the "40 Series", this was first issued in November 1948. The first version—as seen at (11) and (12)—had open rear wheel arches; a plain boot, as seen at (12); and the maker's name, "Vanguard", and

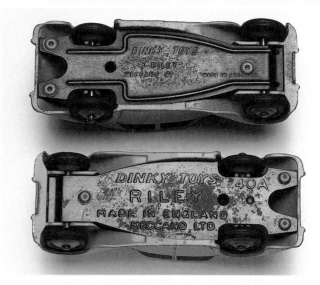

Inset (right): *A view of the differing base plates of the Riley Saloon, DT No 40a (renumbered 158 in 1955); see also notes at (1-4) below. (Top) The tinplate base plate of the first version, issued from July 1947 until 1955, has the maker's and model's names stamped in small letters. (Bottom) On the second version, issued from March 1954 until 1960, the information is stamped in large letters.*

sometimes "40E", stamped on the base in small letters. This version appeared in brown or maroon until April 1950. The second version, finished in fawn or blue, was made between April 1950 and 1955. As seen at (13), it had covered rear wheel housings. The model was renumbered 153 in 1955, and the third version, made from 1954 until 1960, appeared in blue, cream or fawn (14). This had a ridge running horizontally across the boot, base plate information in large letters, and covered rear wheel housings. The first and second versions are not easy to find. Length: 3·583in (91mm).

15 Jaguar XK 120, DT No 157. This was first issued in March 1954 and appeared in green, white or yellow until March 1956. From that date

it was issued in two-tone finish, either cerise-and-turquoise or grey-and-yellow, until production ended in 1962. The two-tone versions are easier to find. Length: 3·819in (97mm).

16 Austin Somerset, DT No 40j. This "40 Series" model first appeared in June 1949 and was made in red or blue, with a base plate stamped with the maker's name, "Austin Somerset" and "40J", until 1955, when it was renumbered 161. It appeared from 1954 until August 1956 in blue only, the base plate carrying the new number. Both versions are of average availability. Length: 3·504in (89mm).

17-18 Rover 75 Saloon, DT No 140b. This model was first issued in April 1951 and was made in maroon (18) only until 1954, when it

was renumbered 156. From May 1954 until January 1956 it was issued in cream (17) only, and from January 1956 until production ended in 1960 in two-tone finish, blue-and-cream or two-tone green. Base plates of the first and second versions are stamped with the maker's name and "Rover 75"; on the third version, the number "156" sometimes appears. Length: 3·976in (101mm).

19-20 Hillman Minx Saloon, DT No 40f. This "40 Series" model was first issued in February 1951 and appeared in light green, dark green, light brown and dark brown until 1955, when it was renumbered 154. From May 1954 until September 1956 it was made in green (19) or brown (20), and from September 1956 until production

ended in 1958 in two-tone finish, either green-and-yellow or cerise-and-blue. Base plate details as (17-18). Length: 3·465in (88mm).

21-22 Morris Oxford Saloon, DT No 40g. First issued in June 1950, this "40 Series" model appeared in green or grey-and-fawn until 1955, when it was renumbered 159. The base plate of the first version is stamped only with the maker's name. From March 1954 until January 1956 it appeared in fawn (21) or green (22), and thereafter, until production ended in 1960, in two-tone finish, either green-and-cream or white-and-red. The base plates of the second and third versions are stamped with the maker's name and "Morris Oxford". The two-tone versions are scarcest. Length: 3·66in (93mm).

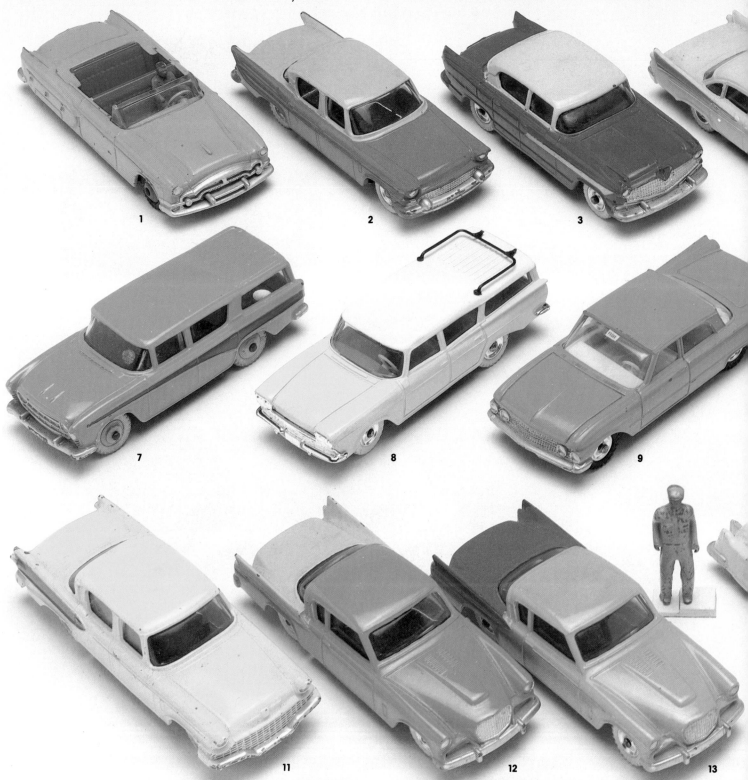

1Packard Convertible by Dinky Toys, Great Britain; Dinky Toys Reference Number (DT No) 132. This model was first issued in November 1955 and remained available until 1961. It was made in fawn, cream or light green body finish and featured a detailed interior, with separately-cast steering wheel and the figure of a driver (left-hand drive),and a plastic windscreen. Its tinplate base is stamped with the maker's name, "132", and "Packard". This is now an item of limited availability. Length: 4·488in (114mm).

2Packard Clipper, DT No 180; first issued in September 1958 and available until 1963. Made in grey-and-orange, fawn-and-pink, and possibly in other colours, it is fitted with windows (which Dinky

then stressed as a special feature, Corgi Toys with windows having been marketed since 1956). The tinplate base bears the maker's name, "180" and "Packard Clipper". Limited. Length: 4·409in (112mm).

3Hudson Hornet, DT No 174; note that the same number was later given to the Ford Mercury Cougar of 1969-72, shown at (10). First issued in August 1958 and available until 1963, this was produced in red-and-cream or yellow-and-grey. It is fitted with windows and its tinplate base is stamped with the maker's name, "174" and "Hudson Hornet". This is a limited item. Length: 4·37in (111mm).

4Dodge Royal Sedan, DT No 191; issued in March 1959 and available until 1964. Made in cream with a brown trim strip or in green with

a black strip, it is fitted with windows. Its tinplate base plate bears the maker's name, "191" and "Dodge Royal Sedan". It may be hard to find. Length: 4·37in (111mm).

5Lincoln Continental, DT No 170; issued in October 1964 and available until 1969. Made in blue-and-white or metallic orange-and-white, it features windows, opening bonnet and boot, jewelled headlights in a chromed radiator and bumper assembly, and a detailed interior. Its diecast base bears the maker's name and "Lincoln Continental". A suspension system is fitted. A limited item. Length: 5in (127mm).

6Ford Thunderbird by Solido, France, dating from 1959. It is interesting to compare this model, featuring a wrap-around windscreen and fitted with a

suspension system, with the Dinky models of US cars shown on this spread. Length: 4·3125in (110mm).

7Nash Rambler, DT No 173; issued in April 1958 and available until 1962. Made in green with a cerise trim strip, or pink with a blue strip, it is fitted with windows. The tinplate base is stamped with the maker's name, "173" and "Nash Rambler". This is a limited item. Length: 3·976in (101mm).

8Rambler Cross-Country Station Wagon, DT No 193; first issued in July 1961 and available until 1968. Produced in yellow-and-white only, this model features a roof-rack, chromed radiator and bumpers, and a detailed interior. It is fitted with a suspension system and the tinplate base plate is stamped with the maker's name, "193"

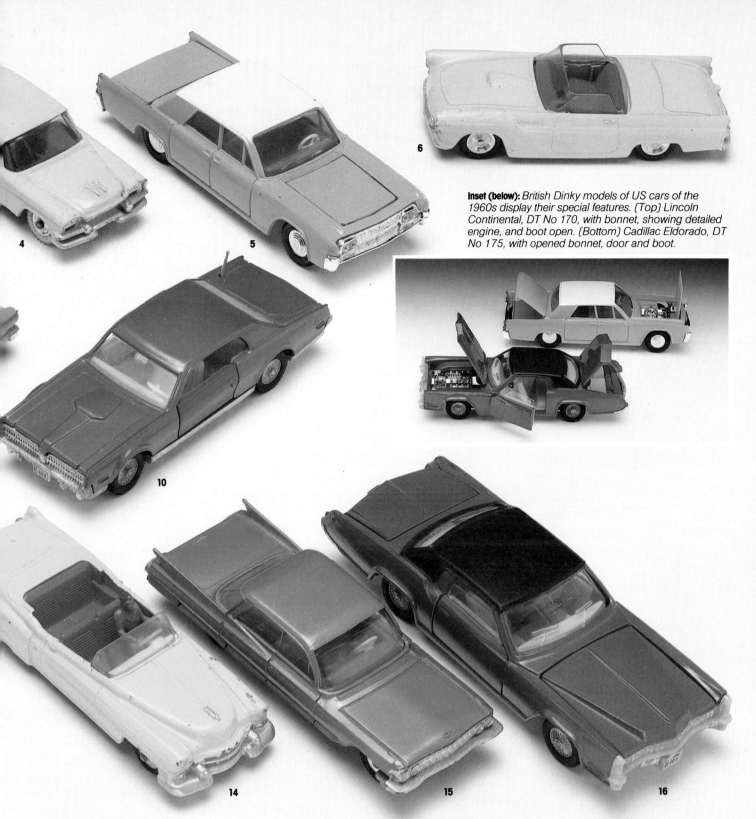

Inset (below): *British Dinky models of US cars of the 1960s display their special features. (Top) Lincoln Continental, DT No 170, with bonnet, showing detailed engine, and boot open. (Bottom) Cadillac Eldorado, DT No 175, with opened bonnet, door and boot.*

and "Rambler Cross-Country". Like most of these models of US cars, it is of limited availability. Length: 4·016in (102mm).

9 Ford Fairlane, DT No 148; first issued in January 1962 and available until 1965. Produced in green body finish only, this model is fitted with windows and has a detailed interior. A suspension system is fitted; the tinplate base plate is stamped with the maker's name, "148" and "Ford Fairlane". Another limited item. Length: 4·37in (111mm).

10 Ford Mercury Cougar, DT No 174; first issued in 1969 and available until 1972. This model was made only in blue finish and features opening doors, a radio aerial, and seats. It is fitted with suspension and speedwheels and has a diecast

base. The model is fairly common. Length: 4·803in (122mm).

11 Studebaker President, DT No 179; first issued in October 1958 and available until 1963. This model was produced in yellow with a blue trim strip, or in blue with a dark blue trim strip. Windows are fitted, but there is no interior detail. The tinplate base is stamped with the maker's name, "179" and "Studebaker President". This is one of the less common models of its period. Length: 4·252in (108mm).

12-13 Studebaker Golden Hawk, DT No. 169; first issued in November 1958, this model remained available until 1963. It was produced only in the colour schemes shown here: green-and-fawn (12) or fawn-and-red (13). The

model is fitted with windows but has no interior detail. The tinplate base plate is stamped with the maker's name, "169" and "Studebaker Golden Hawk". Limited. Length: 4·17in (106mm).

14 Cadillac Eldorado, DT No 131. This model—for a later version of the same car, see (16)—was first issued in June 1956, and remained available until 1963. It appeared in yellow, pink or fawn body finish. It has a plastic windscreen, a detailed interior with a separately-cast steering wheel and the figure of a driver (left-hand drive), an opening boot and spoked wheels. The tinplate base is stamped with the maker's name, "131" and "Cadillac Eldorado". Its availability is limited. Length: 4·646in (118mm).

15 Cadillac 62, DT No 147; first issued in October 1962, when it was priced at 4s 11d (24½p, 29c), and available until 1968. It was made in metallic green finish only, and has windows, a detailed interior and a suspension system. The tinplate base is stamped with the maker's name, "147" and "Cadillac". Another limited item. Length: 4·449in (113mm).

16 Cadillac Eldorado, DT No 175; first issued in 1969 and available until 1972. This large and impressive model was produced in purple-and-black (as shown) and possibly in other colours. It features opening doors, boot and bonnet and a detailed interior, and is fitted with a suspension system and speedwheels. It is fairly common. Length: 5·236in (133mm).

Diecast Cars by Dinky Toys, Great Britain, 1956-1972

1 Hillman Minx by Dinky Toys, Great Britain; Dinky Toys Reference Number (DT No) 175. This model was first issued in August 1958 and remained available until 1961. Appearing in grey-and-blue (as shown) or pink-and-green finish, it is fitted with windows. Its tinplate base is stamped with the maker's name and "Hillman Minx". It is now of limited availability. Length: 3·465in (88mm).

2 Hillman Imp; DT No 138, issued in November 1963 and available until 1972. Made in metallic green or blue, it features windows, a detailed interior, an opening bonnet (with engine detail) and an opening boot (with luggage). A suspension system is fitted. Its diecast base bears the maker's name, "138" and "Hillman Imp".

This is a fairly common item. Length: 3·386in (86mm).

3 Ford Capri; DT No 143, issued in August 1962 and available until 1966. Made in green-and-white only, it features windows, interior detail, suspension and fingertip steering. Its tinplate base is stamped with the maker's name, "143" and "Ford Capri". Fairly common. Length: 3·5625in (90mm).

4 Ford Consul Corsair; DT No 130, issued in June 1964 and available until 1968. Made in blue, red, and possibly other colours, it has sliding windows, interior detail, opening bonnet (with engine) and jewelled headlights. Suspension is fitted and the diecast base bears the maker's name, "130" and "Ford Corsair". Its availability is now limited. Length: 4·17in (106mm).

5 Ford Cortina; DT No 139, issued in June 1963 and available until 1964. Made in metallic blue only, it features windows, interior detail, opening doors, suspension and fingertip steering. Its tinplate base bears the maker's name, "139" and "Ford Cortina". Limited. Length: 4·016in (102mm).

6-7 Austin A105; DT No 176, issued in August 1958 and available until 1963. It is known to have appeared in cream with a blue strip, as at (6), or grey with red strip; a two-tone variant is shown at (7). This was the first Dinky car to be fitted with windows, but it has no interior detail. Its tinplate base bears the maker's name, "176" and "Austin A105". Limited. Length: 4·016in (102mm).

8 Triumph 2000; DT No 135, issued

in November 1963 and available until 1968. Made in blue-and-white, as seen, and possibly in other colours, it features windows, interior detail, opening doors, bonnet (with engine) and boot (with luggage), suspension and fingertip steering. Its diecast base bears the maker's name, "135" and "Triumph 2000". Limited. Length: 4·134in (105mm).

9 Triumph Vitesse; DT No 134, issued in November 1963 and available until 1968. Made in metallic green or blue, it features windows, interior detail and suspension. Its tinplate base bears the maker's name, "134" and "Triumph Vitesse". Limited. Length: 3·425in (87mm).

10 Triumph 1300; DT No 162, issued in 1966 and available until 1969.

It features windows, interior detail, jewelled headlights, opening bonnet (with engine) and boot, and suspension with fingertip steering. Its base is diecast. Limited. Length: 3·622in (92mm).

11 Vauxhall Viva; DT No 136, issued in May 1964 and available until 1972. Made in blue or white, it features windows, interior detail, opening bonnet (with engine) and boot, and suspension with fingertip steering. Its diecast base bears the maker's name, "136" and "Vauxhall Viva". Fairly common. Length: 3·66in (93mm).

12 Vauxhall Cresta; DT No 164, issued in March 1957 and available until 1960. Made in green-and-grey or maroon-and-cream, it has neither windows nor interior detail. Its tinplate base bears the maker's name,

"164" and "Vauxhall Cresta". Fairly scarce. Length: 3·78in (96mm).

13 Vauxhall Victor Estate Car; DT No 141, issued in April 1963 and available until 1967. Made in yellow only, it features windows, interior detail, an opening tailgate, and suspension with fingertip steering. Its tinplate base bears the maker's name, "141" and "Victor Estate". Fairly common. Length: 3·622in (92mm).

14 Volkswagen 1500; DT No 144, issued in March 1963 and available until 1966. Made in white only, it features windows, interior detail (left-hand drive), opening bonnet (with plastic luggage), and suspension with fingertip steering. Its tinplate base bears the maker's name, "144" and "VW 1500". Fairly common. Length: 3·66in (93mm).

15 Volkswagen; DT No 181, issued in February 1956 and available until 1969. Made in blue, grey or green, it has neither windows nor interior detail. Its tinplate base bears the maker's name, "Volkswagen" and, sometimes, the number "181". A limited item. Length: 3·5625in (90mm).

16 Volkswagen Karmann Ghia Coupé; DT No 187, issued in November 1959 and available until 1963. Made in green-and-cream or red-and-black, it features windows and suspension. Its tinplate base bears the maker's name and "Volkswagen Karmann Ghia". Fairly common. Length: 3·78in (96mm).

17 Volvo 122S; DT No 184, issued in December 1961 and available until 1964. Made in red only, it has windows, interior detail and

suspension. Its tinplate base bears the maker's name, "184" and "Volvo 122S". Fairly common. Length: 3·858in (98mm).

18 Opel Kapitan; DT No 177, issued in August 1961 and available until 1967. Made in blue only, it has windows, interior detail, and suspension with fingertip steering. Its tinplate base bears the maker's name and "Opel Kapitan". Limited. Length: 3·937in (100mm).

19 Daimler V.8 2½ Litre; DT No 146, issued in January 1963 and available until 1966. Made in metallic green only, it features windows, interior detail, and suspension with fingertip steering. Its tinplate base bears the maker's name and "Daimler 2.5 litre". This is now a fairly scarce item. Length: 3·74in (95mm).

1 2 3 4

7 8 9 10

16

13 14 15

1 Hillman Minx by Dinky Toys, Great Britain; Dinky Toys Reference Number (DT No) 175, first issued in August 1958 and available until 1961. Appearing in pink-and-green or grey-and-blue finish, this has clear plastic windows but no interior detail. It has a tinplate base and detachable rubber tyres. A fairly scarce item. Length: 3·465in (88mm).

2 Singer Vogue by Dinky Toys, Great Britain; DT No 145, issued in December 1962 and available until 1966. Appearing only in metallic green, it has windows and a detailed interior and features suspension and "fingertip steering". It has a tinplate base and detachable rubber tyres. Limited. Length: 3·66in (93mm).

3 Singer Gazelle by Dinky Toys, Great Britain; DT No 168, issued in January 1959 and available until

1963. Appearing in cream-and-brown or grey-and-green, it has windows but no interior detail. It has a tinplate base and detachable tyres. Scarce. Length: 3·622in (92mm).

4 Sunbeam Rapier by Dinky Toys, Great Britain; DT No 166, issued in June 1958 and available until 1963. Appearing in two-tone blue or cream-and-orange, it has windows but no interior detail. The base is tinplate and it has detachable rubber tyres. A fairly scarce item. Length: 3·504in (89mm).

5 Ford Zephyr by Dinky Toys, Great Britain; DT No 162, issued in April 1956 and available until 1960. Appearing in cream-and-green or two-tone blue, it has a tinplate base and is fitted with detachable rubber tyres. A scarce item. Length: 3·78in (96mm).

6 Jaguar 3.4-litre Mark II by Dinky Toys, Great Britain; DT No 195, issued in August 1960 and available until 1966. Appearing in maroon, cream or grey, it has windows, a detailed interior, suspension with fingertip steering, and detachable rubber tyres. Its base is tinplate. Scarce. Length: 3·819in (97mm).

7 Riley Pathfinder by Corgi Toys, Great Britain; maker's reference number 205, available 1956-61. Appearing in red or blue, this has windows but no interior detail. It is fairly scarce: a version with friction wheel motion, available only until 1959, is even harder to find. Length: 3·819in (97mm).

8 Ford Consul by Corgi Toys, Great Britain; maker's reference number 200, available 1956-59. The version shown, which appeared in blue or

green finish, has friction wheel motion. It is fairly scarce, and a little harder to find than a version without friction wheel motion that appeared in a number of body colours from 1956 until 1961. Length: 3·565in (90mm).

9 Humber Hawk by Dinky Toys, Great Britain; DT No 165, issued in July 1959 and available until 1963. Appearing in green-and-black or maroon-and-fawn, it is fitted with windows and has a tinplate base and detachable rubber tyres. Fairly scarce. Length: 4·016in (102mm).

10 Alfa Romeo 1900 Super Sprint by Dinky Toys, Great Britain; DT No 185, issued in January 1961 and available until 1963. Appearing in red or yellow, it has windows, a detailed interior (left-hand drive) and suspension. It has a tinplate

base and detachable rubber tyres. Limited. Length: 4·016in (102mm).

11 Jaguar Mark 10 by Dinky Toys, Great Britain; DT No 142, issued in November 1962 and available until 1968. Appearing only in metallic blue, it has windows, a detailed interior and an opening boot (with luggage). It is fitted with suspension and has a tinplate base and rubber tyres. Limited availability. Length: 4·17in (106mm).

12 Plymouth Fury Sports by Dinky Toys, Great Britain; DT No 115, available 1967-68. This model has cast figures of driver (left-hand drive) and passenger, a clear plastic windscreen and a detailed interior, an opening bonnet, twin rear aerials, and suspension. Limited. Length: 4·803in (122mm).

13 Ford Corsair 2000E by Dinky Toys,

Great Britain; DT No 169, available 1967-69. Appearing only in silver-and-black, this has windows, a detailed interior, opening bonnet, and suspension with fingertip steering. Limited. Length: 4·252in (108mm).

14 Ford Cortina Rally Car by Dinky Toys, Great Britain; DT No 212, available 1967-69. Appearing only as shown, in white-and-black, with "Castrol" and "East African Safari" transfers and the race number "8", this features a plated roof-mounted spotlight, opening doors, a detailed interior and suspension. Limited. Length: 4·016in (102mm).

15 Ford Escort by Dinky Toys, Great Britain; DT No 168, available 1968-76. Appearing in blue or red, this features opening doors, bonnet and boot, and a detailed interior with tilting seats. This is a late

production version with plastic wheels. Length: 3·819in (97mm).

16 Fiat 2000 Station Wagon by Dinky Toys, Great Britain; DT No 172, available 1965-68. It has an opening bonnet and tailgate, a detailed interior (left-hand drive) with tilting seats, and suspension. Limited. Length: 4·252in (108mm).

17 Lincoln Continental by Dinky Toys, Great Britain; DT No 170, issued in October 1964 and available until 1969. It has a chromed radiator and bumpers, an opening bonnet (with chromed engine), opening boot, detailed interior (left-hand drive), and suspension. Its base is diecast. Limited. Length: 5in (127mm).

18 Ford Mustang by Dinky Toys, Great Britain; DT No 161, available 1965-72. Appearing in white or yellow, this has an opening bonnet (with

detailed engine), doors and boot, jewelled headlights, a detailed interior with tilting seats, and a suspension system. Limited. Length: 4·37in (111mm).

19 Opel Commodore by Dinky Toys, Great Britain; DT No 179, available 1971-74. This model has an opening bonnet (with detailed engine) and doors, a detailed interior (left-hand drive) with tilting seats, and suspension. A fairly common item. Length: 4·21in (107mm).

Inset (top right): *Dinky cars shown on this spread display their special features. (Left to right; top to bottom): Lincoln Continental (17); Ford Mustang (18); Opel Commodore (19); Ford Corsair 2000E (13); Ford Cortina (14); Ford Escort (15); Jaguar Mark 10 (11).*

1 Ford Vedette (1953 Model) by Dinky Toys, France; French Dinky Toys Reference Number (FDT No) 24x. This model was first issued in 1954 and remained available until 1956. Finished in grey, it has neither windows nor interior detail. It was also available in a taxi version (FDT No 24xt). Length: 4·134in (105mm).

2 Ford Vedette (1949 Model); FDT No 24q, first issued in 1950 and available until 1955. The first model of a Ford car to be issued by Dinky Toys, France, this may be found with a number of variations to its tinplate base. Length: 3·937in (100mm).

3 Panhard PL17 Saloon; FDT No 547, first issued in 1960 and available until 1968. Three versions of this model were made:

in the first two types, the door handles are so positioned as to suggest that the doors (non-opening on the model) open from front to back; in the third version, as seen here, the door handles are correctly placed. Finished in red, this model features windows and a detailed interior, including steering wheel (left-hand drive). A suspension system is fitted. Length: 4·17in (106mm).

4-5 Peugeot 203 Sedan; FDT No 24r. This model first appeared in 1954; it was renumbered 533 in 1959 and was deleted from the range in the same year. Shown here in green (4) and blue (5) finish, this model appeared in three versions, the major variations being in the size of the rear window. The model at (4) is an early version, with a

small rear window; that at (5) is a later type, with a large rear window (the difference is just apparent in the photograph). Note also that (4) has painted wheels, whereas (5) has plated wheels. Length: 3·858in (98mm).

6 Peugeot 403 UF Estate Car; FDT No 24f. This model was first issued in 1958 and remained available until 1962. Finished in pale blue, it has neither windows nor interior detail. Length: 4·17in (106mm).

7 Peugeot 403 Saloon; FDT No 521, dating from 1960. Note that this model, finished in grey, is fitted with windows and that the casting incorporates a sun-roof. See also (8). Length: 4·09in (104mm).

8 Peugeot 403 Saloon; FDT No 24b, dating from 1956. This model is almost identical with (7), but

is not fitted with windows. Length: 4·09in (104mm).

9 Simca Aronde; FDT No 544, dating from 1959. In two-tone finish, maroon with a white roof and with a silver body trim strip, this model is fitted with windows. Length: 3·8125in (97mm).

10-12 Simca 9 Aronde; FDT No 24u. This model was first issued in 1953; it was renumbered 536 in 1959 and was deleted from the range in the same year. It appeared in three versions, of which two are shown here. The models at (10) and (12), finished in green and grey respectively, are of the first type, issued in 1953-55: in comparison with (11), note the different radiator grille and the painted wheels of (10) and (12). The model at (11) is of the third

5

6

7

8

13

14

15

16

20

21

22

type, issued in 1958-59; it is in two-tone finish, grey with a green roof, and has chromed wheels. Length: 3·66in (93mm).

13 Simca Chambord; FDT No 24k. This model was first issued in 1959 and was renumbered 528 in the same year. It remained available until 1961. Seen here in a two-tone finish—dark green lower body and roof and pale green upper body—it is fitted with plastic windows but has no interior detail. Length: 4·252in (108mm).

14 Simca Versailles; FDT No 24z. This model was first issued in 1956; it was renumbered 541 in 1969 and remained available until 1960. In two-tone finish, blue with a white roof, this model has neither windows nor interior detail. Length: 4·055in (103mm).

15 Renault Dauphine; FDT No 24e, dating from 1957. Finished in green, this is another simple model, without windows or interior detail. Length: 3·5625in (90mm).

16 Renault Floride Coupé, FDT No 543, first issued in 1960 and available until 1963. Finished in gold, this model features plastic windows and a suspension system. Length: 3·819in (97mm).

17-18 Citroën DS19, FDT No 24c. This model was first issued in 1956; it was renumbered 522 in 1959 and remained available until 1968—obviously a most popular model of a famous car of innovatory design. As seen in the two versions in two-tone finish—white-and-black and cream-and-black—shown here, it was originally issued, from 1956 to 1957, without windows.

It appeared with plastic windows from 1958-59 onward, and subsequently underwent other improvements. On the two examples shown, note that (17) has concave wheels and that (18) has ridged wheels. Length: 4·375in (111mm).

19-20 Citroën 11BL; FDT No 24n. This model was first issued in 1949 and remained available until 1955. Two versions are shown: the car in grey finish at (19) is of the later type, issued in 1953-55; the casting incorporates a boot and it has a plain radiator. The car in black finish at (20) is of the earlier type, issued in 1949-51, without a boot, but with a cast-on spare wheel (the edge just visible at the rear of the car in this photograph), a tinplate front bumper and a detailed radiator.

Lengths (19): 4·17in (106mm); (20): 3·75in (95mm).

21-22 Citroën 2CV (1950 Model); FDT No 24t. This model was first issued in 1952, renumbered 535 in 1959, and remained available until 1963—another long-lived model of a French car that has inspired worldwide affection. The two examples shown, in different two-tone finishes, are early versions, lacking windows and interior detail. Note that (21) has ridged wheels and that (22) has concave wheels. A later, improved version (FDT No 535), appearing in 1962 and fitted with windows and a suspension system, was issued under the same reference number in Great Britain in 1962, remaining available until 1965. Length: 3·465in (88mm).

1 Fiat 2300 Coupé by Norev, France; maker's reference number 702, dating from 1965. The model has a detailed moulded interior, with tilting seats and steering column (left-hand drive, like all other cars with interior detail shown on this spread). It has opening doors and is fitted with a suspension system. The base is plastic. Length: 4·409in (112mm).

2 Alfa-Romeo 1900 Super Sprint Coupé by Dinky Toys, France; French Dinky Toys Reference Number (FDT No) 24j, dating from 1959. It has windows but no interior detail. Length: 4in (102mm).

3 Volkswagen Karmann Ghia Coupé by Dinky Toys, France; FDT No 24m, dating from 1959. Again, with windows but no interior detail. Length: 3·75in (95mm).

4 Volkswagen 1500 Karmann Ghia by Corgi Toys, Great Britain; maker's reference number 239. This model was made between 1963 and 1968; seen here in cream finish, it was produced also in red. It features an opening bonnet and boot (with plastic detail inside), clear plastic windows, a detailed moulded interior, a suspension system and a detachable spare wheel. This model should be quite easy to find. Length: 3·583in (91mm).

5-7 Citroën DS 19 (1955 Model) by Dinky Toys, France; FDT No 24c. This model was originally issued in 1956-57, without the windows seen on the three examples here. The three cars shown, in two-tone colour variations, are examples of the second version, with windows —and note that (7) is fitted with concave wheels—issued in 1958-59. The model was renumbered 522 in 1959 and remained in production until 1968. For an improved model of the same car, see (8). Length: 4·375in (111mm).

8 Citroën DS 19 (1955 Model) by Dinky Toys, France; FDT No 530. This improved version of the model shown at (5-7) was first issued in 1963 and remained in production until 1970. In comparison with (5-7), note the opening bonnet and boot (with detachable spare wheel visible), the fully moulded interior complete with steering column, and the jewelled headlights. It has a diecast base and is fitted with a suspension system. Length: 4·375in (111mm).

9 Peugeot 504 Cabriolet by Dinky Toys, France; FDT No 1423. This model was first issued in 1969 and remained in production until 1971. Well-detailed, it features an operating Ackerman steering system. The base is plastic. The plastic windscreen of this model is very fragile. Length: 3·875in (98mm).

10 Peugeot 404 Saloon by Dinky Toys, France; FDT No 553. This model was issued with the same reference number by Dinky Toys, Great Britain, first appearing in 1962 and available, in green body finish in Britain, until 1965. It has a moulded interior complete with steering column, windows and a suspension system. The tinplate base is stamped with the maker's name, "Peugeot 404", "1/43" (scale), "61" (year of issue in France), and "553". Length: 4·016in (102mm).

11 Peugeot 204 Coupé by Norev,

5

6

7

8

13

14

15

19

20

21

France; maker's reference number 801, dating from 1968. This has an opening bonnet and doors, windscreen, and a moulded plastic interior with tilting seats. The base is plastic and suspension is fitted. Length: 3·31in (84mm).

12 Peugeot 404 Shooting Brake by Dinky Toys, France; FDT No 525, dating from 1964. Its most notable features are the opening tailgate and fold-down rear seat. It has windows and a detailed moulded interior. Suspension is fitted. Length: 4·125in (105mm).

13 Peugeot 204 Saloon by Dinky Toys, France; FDT No 510, dating from 1965. Finished in white, this model features an opening bonnet that reveals engine detail. It has a windscreen that includes detail of a rear-view mirror and

a moulded interior. Note that the body casting incorporates a sun-roof, as on the Peugeot 404 at (10). It has a diecast base and a suspension system is fitted. Length: 3·5in (89mm).

14 Citroën "Le Dandy" Coupé by Corgi Toys, Great Britain; maker's reference number 259. This was first issued in 1966 and appeared in maroon or blue body finish until production ceased in 1969. This model of a car in which Citroën mounted a Henri Chapron body on the DS chassis features an opening bonnet and doors, jewelled lights, plastic windows, and a detailed moulded interior with tilting seats. It has a diecast chassis and suspension is fitted. It may prove a little harder to find than the Volkswagen 1500 shown at (4).

Length: 4·016in (102mm).

15 Citroën 3CV by Dinky Toys, France; FDT No 557, dating from 1962. This model features an opening bonnet and boot, windows, and a detailed moulded interior. Length: 3·56in (90mm).

16-17 Mercedes 190SL by Dinky Toys, France; FDT No 24h. Two examples are shown: the model at (16), dating from 1960, has windows; the earlier version at (17), dating from 1958, has not. Length: 3·875in (98mm).

18 Mercedes Benz 300SE by Dinky Toys, France; FDT No 533, dating from 1963. It has windows and a detailed interior and is fitted with suspension. Length: 4·5in (114mm).

19 Mercedes Benz 230SL by Dinky Toys, France; FDT No 516, dating from 1964. It has a bonnet that

opens to show engine detail, an opening boot, and a detailed interior with tilting seats. Its most notable feature is a detachable hardtop. It has a diecast base and a suspension system is fitted. Length: 3·875in (98mm).

20 Borgward Isabella by Dinky Toys, France; FDT No 549, dating from 1961. Finished in silver, the model has windows and a detailed moulded interior. Suspension is fitted. Length: 4in (102mm).

21 Daf Saloon by Dinky Toys, France; FDT No 508, dating from 1966. Finished in cream, this model features a detailed moulded interior that includes the plastic figure of a driver. It has opening doors and jewelled headlights. The base is diecast and suspension is fitted. Length: 3·25in (83mm).

1 Chevrolet Corvair by Dinky Toys, France; French Dinky Toys Reference Number (FDT No) 552, dating from 1961. Finished in red, this model features windows and a detailed moulded interior with steering wheel (left-hand drive). It is fitted with a suspension system and has "fingertip steering". Length: 4·125in (105mm).

2 Studebaker Commander Coupé; FDT No 24y, first issued in 1955. This model was renumbered 540 in 1959 and remained available until 1961. The example shown is of the earlier type. It is finished in pale grey with a maroon roof and has no windows or interior detail. In the later type, the lower parts of the front wings and doors were finished in the same colour as the roof. Length: 4·25in (108mm).

3 Ford Thunderbird Convertible; FDT No 555, dating from 1961. The identical model, under the same reference number and in the original French packaging, was marketed in Great Britain from July 1962—when eleven other models of French origin, including the Chrysler Saratoga shown at (19), also appeared in Britain—until 1965. It was priced in Britain at 7s 8d (38½p, 46c). The model was made only with a white body. It features a detailed moulded plastic interior, with a separately-cast steering wheel and the figure of a driver (left-hand drive), and a plastic windscreen. With a suspension system and "fingertip steering", it has a tinplate base plate stamped with the maker's name, "Ford Thunderbird", "1/43" (scale),

"61" (year of French issue), and "555". This is a model with limited availability in Britain. Length: 4·764in (121mm).

4-5 Ford Galaxie 500; FDT No 1402, dating from 1968. This model, shown here in two finishes—fawn with maroon interior (4); black with cream interior (5)—features opening doors, bonnet and boot, windows (incorporating detail of rear-view mirror), and a detailed interior. The base is diecast. Length: 4·875in (124mm).

6-7 Ford Thunderbird Coupé; FDT No 1419, dating from 1969. Shown here in two finishes—metallic green (6) and metallic green with a black roof (7), in both cases with cream interior—this model features windows and a detailed interior. The base is made of plastic.

Length: 4·6875in (119mm).

8-9 De Soto 59 Diplomat; FDT No 545, dating from 1960. This model, shown in two finishes—green with cream roof (8) and orange with black roof (9), in both cases with a silver body trim strip—is fitted with windows, but it features no interior detail: Length: 4·4375in (113mm).

10-11 Lincoln Premier; FDT No 532, first issued in 1959 and available until 1965. This model, again shown in two finishes—blue with a silver roof (10) and pale green with a dark green roof (11)—is fitted with windows but has no interior detail. Length: 4·6875in (119mm).

12-13 Buick Roadmaster; FDT No 24v. This model was first issued in 1954; it was renumbered 538 in 1959, but was deleted from the

range in the same year. Shown here in two finishes—cream with a green roof (12) and light blue with a dark blue roof (13)—it has neither windows nor interior detail, but the casting incorporates a red-enamelled mascot on the bonnet. Length: 4·375in (111mm).
14-15 Plymouth Belvedere Coupé; FDT No 24d. This model was first issued in 1957; it was renumbered 523 in 1959 and was deleted from the range in 1961. Again, it is shown in two different finishes— grey, with a red trim area on the lower body and a red roof (14); green, with a black trim area on the lower body and a black roof (15). The model has neither windows nor interior detail, but the casting incorporates a plated mascot on the bonnet.

Length: 4·3125in (110mm).
16-18 Chrysler New Yorker Convertible (1955 Model); FDT No 24a. This model was first issued in 1956; it was renumbered 520 in 1959 and was deleted from the range in 1961. Three examples are shown here, marking both variations in finish—yellow with green interior (16); red with cream interior (17-18)—and, particularly, the variation in the radiator grille between (16-17) and (18). The model features a plastic windscreen and a detailed interior complete with steering wheel (left-hand drive). The casting incorporates a silver-finished mascot on the bonnet. Length: 4·3125in (110mm).
19 Chrysler Saratoga; FDT No 550, first issued in France in 1960

and remaining available in that country until 1966. The identical model, under the same reference number and in its original French packaging, was marketed in Great Britain, where it was initially priced at 7s 8d (38½p, 46c), from 1962 until 1965. As noted at (3), besides this model and the Ford Thunderbird Convertible shown at (3), ten other models from the French Dinky factory were released in Great Britain at this time. They were (with FDT No in each case): Renault 4L (518); 2CV Citroën (535); Peugeot 404 (553); Citroën Delivery Van "Cibié" (561; a later version, "Glaces Gervais", was marketed only in France); Estafette Renault (Renault Pick-Up) (563); Panhard Armoured Car (815); A.M.X. 13-Ton Tank (817); M3 Half-

Track (822); Brockway Military Truck with Pontoon Bridge (884); and Unic Tractor and Boilot Car Transporter Trailer (894). This model of the Chrysler Saratoga was produced only in pink-and-white finish, as shown here; it features windows and a detailed interior with a separately-cast steering wheel (left-hand drive). With a suspension system and "fingertip steering" (called "Prestomatic" in Great Britain), it has a tinplate base plate stamped with the maker's name, "Chrysler Saratoga", "1/43", "61", and "550". This model is perhaps a little easier to find in Britain than the Ford Thunderbird Convertible, with similar production history, shown at (3). Length: 5·079in (129mm).

1 Renault 4L "P&T" by Dinky Toys, France; French Dinky Toys Reference Number (FDT No) 561, dating from 1972. With a body finished in yellow, this model features windows and a detailed moulded interior complete with steering column (left-hand drive, like all the other models with interior detail shown on this spread). It has a plastic base and suspension is fitted. Note the provision of number plates on this and some of the other French Dinky Toys shown on this spread. Length: 3·346in (85mm).

2 Renault 4L "Depannage Autoroutes"; FDT No 518, dating from 1970. The identical model, still in its French packaging, was issued under the same reference number by Dinky Toys, Great Britain,

in July 1962; it remained available in Britain until 1965. The model was boxed with a road sign (not shown here). Finished in orange, this model features a plastic whip-aerial, plastic windows, a detailed moulded interior, and "fingertip steering" (Called "Prestomatic" by the British factory) with a suspension system. It has a tinplate base on which is stamped the maker's name, "Renault 4L", and "518". Length: 3·346in (85mm).

3 Renault 6; FDT No 1416, dating from 1969. Finished in red, this model features opening front doors, windows, and a detailed moulded interior. It has a plastic base and suspension is fitted. Length: 3·5in (89mm).

4 Renault 12 Gordini; FDT No

1424g, dating from 1971. Finished in blue with white side stripes, this model features windows—note the detail of the rear-view mirror, as on some other models shown on this spread—opening doors and a detailed moulded interior. It has a plastic base and suspension is fitted. Length: 4·8125in (122mm).

5 Renault R8; FDT No 103 (Junior), dating from 1964. Finished in red, this is a simple model, without interior detail or windows, using the same body casting as the more detailed car shown at (6). Length: 3·474in (88mm).

6 Renault R8 Gordini; FDT No 1414, dating from 1969. In blue-and-white rally finish with the race number "36", this model features a detailed moulded interior that

includes the figure of a driver, windows, and jewelled headlights. A suspension system is fitted. Length: 3·474in (88mm).

7 Simca 1500 GLS Shooting Brake; FDT No 507, dating from 1967. Finished in dark grey, this features opening front doors and tailgate, windows (including sliding side windows), and a detailed moulded interior that includes a removable picnic table (as shown here). Length: 3·75in (95mm).

8 Peugeot 404; FDT No 101 (Junior), dating from 1963. Finished in orange, this lacks windows and interior detail. Note that the same body casting, with sun-roof, is used for the more detailed car at (12). Length: 4in (102mm).

9 Peugeot 404 Pininfarina; DT No 528, introduced in 1966 and

4   5   6   7

11   12   13   14

18   19   20   21

deleted in 1971. Finished in blue, this well-detailed model features jewelled headlights, a plastic windshield, and a detailed moulded interior that includes the plastic figure of a lady driver. It has a diecast base and suspension is fitted. Length: 4in (102mm).

10 Peugeot 204 Cabriolet; DT No 511, dating from 1968. Finished in pale blue, this model features opening doors and bonnet, a well-modelled plastic windscreen, and a detailed moulded interior with tilting seats. It has a diecast base. Length: 3·3125in (84mm).

11 Peugeot 404 Shooting Brake; FDT No 525, dating from 1964. Finished in cream, this model features windows, jewelled headlights, an opening tailgate, and a detailed moulded interior that

includes a fold-down rear seat. A suspension system is fitted. Length: 4·125in (105mm).

12 Peugeot 404; FDT No 536, dating from 1965. Finished in red, this model—shown here with the plastic Monoroute (Trailer), FDT No 812—features windows, a detailed moulded interior, and a body casting that incorporates a sun-roof. A suspension system is fitted. Length: 4in (102mm).

13 Simca 1000; FDT No 519, dating from 1963. Finished in blue, this model features windows and a detailed moulded interior. A suspension system is fitted. Length: 3·375in (86mm).

14 Simca 1000; FDT No 104 (Junior), dating from 1964. Finished in light green, this is the simpler version of the model at (13),

without windows or interior detail. Length: 3·375in (86mm).

15 Fiat 600; FDT No 520, dating from 1963. Finished in red, this diminutive model features windows, a detailed moulded interior, and suspension. Length: 3in (76mm).

16 Fiat 1800 Estate Car; FDT No 548, dating from 1960. In two-tone finish of cream-and-gold, this model features windows, a detailed moulded interior, and suspension. Length: 4in (102mm).

17 Fiat 1200 Grande Vue; FDT No 531, dating from 1959. In two-tone gold-and-white, this car has windows but lacks any interior detail. Length: 3·5in (89mm).

18 Panhard 24; FDT No 524, dating from 1964. Finished in dark grey, this has slide-down side windows and a detailed moulded

interior. Suspension is fitted. Length: 3·8125in (97mm).

19 Opel Admiral; FDT No 513, dating from 1966. Finished in red, this has an opening bonnet and boot and a detailed moulded interior. It has a diecast base and suspension is fitted. Length: 4·48in (114mm).

20 Opel Rekord; FDT No 554, dating from 1961. In two-tone fawn-and-white, this has windows and a detailed moulded interior. Note "Rekord" incorporated into the body casting on the right rear wing. A suspension system is fitted. Length: 4·06in (103mm).

21 Opel Kadett Saloon; FDT No 540, dating from 1963. Finished in red, it has slide-down side windows and a detailed moulded interior. A suspension system is fitted. Length: 3·5in (89mm).

1Citroën 2CV by Dinky Toys, Spain; Spanish Dinky Toys Reference Number (SDT No) 500, dating from the 1970s. Finished in orange, this model features an open sun-roof, an opening bonnet, and a basically-detailed interior (left-hand drive; like all the cars shown on this spread) of moulded plastic. It is fitted with a metal base. Length: 3·425in (87mm).

2Citroën Dyane by Dinky Toys, Spain; SDT No 1413, dating from the 1970s. Finished in light grey, this model has a matt-finished roof, a non-opening bonnet, clear plastic windows and a detailed interior. It has a plastic base. Length: 3·504in (89mm).

3Citroën DS23 by Dinky Toys, Spain; SDT No 530, dating from the 1970s. Finished in metallic maroon

with a black roof, this model has headlights with clear plastic lenses, opening doors and a detailed interior. It is fitted with a metal base. Length: 4·252in (108mm).

4Citroën CX Pallas by Dinky Toys, Spain; SDT No 1455, dating from the 1970s. Finished in metallic mid-blue, this has headlights with clear plastic lenses, opening doors and a detailed interior. Like a number of the other Spanish-made Dinky cars shown on this spread, it is fitted with number plates—and these may vary in different examples of the same model (see *Inset, above right*). It is fitted with a metal base. Length: 4·016in (102mm).

5Renault 6 by Dinky Toys, Spain; SDT No 1453, dating from the 1970s. Finished in grey, this model

features opening doors, clear plastic windscreen (the windscreen incorporating detail of a rear-view mirror; a feature noticeable on several other cars on this spread), and a detailed interior. It has a plastic base. Length: 3·504in (89mm).

6Volkswagen Scirocco by Dinky Toys, Spain; SDT No 1539, dating from the 1970s. Finished in metallic light green, this model has clear plastic windows, a detailed interior and a base made of metal. Length: 3·504in (89mm).

7Renault 4L by Dinky Toys, Spain; SDT No 518, dating from the 1970s. Finished in powder blue, this model has clear plastic windows, a detailed interior and a plastic base. Length: 3·307in (84mm).

8Renault 17TS by Dinky Toys, Spain; SDT No 1451, dating

from the 1970s. Finished in yellow, this model features opening doors, a tinted plastic windscreen and a detailed interior of moulded plastic. It has a metal base. Length: 4·17in (106mm).

9Renault 4L by Dinky Toys, Spain; SDT No 518, dating from the 1970s. Finished in medium blue, but otherwise identical with (7); a variation in body colour finish. Length: 3·307in (84mm).

10Matra Simca Bagheera by Dinky Toys, Spain; SDT No 1454, dating from the 1970s. Finished in light green, with a matt black rear panel, this model has a tinted plastic windscreen and a detailed interior. It is fitted with a metal base. Length: 3·5625in (90mm).

11Simca 1100 by Dinky Toys, Spain; SDT No 1407, dating from the

Inset (right): *Closeup front views of the Peugeot 204 by Dinky Toys, Spain, SDT No 510, shown also at (12) below. Note the variation in the number plates fitted to these otherwise identical models: "5359 TV 75" on the example to the left; "3978 AD 93" on the car to the right. The photograph shows the well-modelled radiator with marque badge; the clear plastic lenses of the headlights; the basic engine detail revealed by the open bonnet (left); and the details of wipers and mirror on the windscreen (right).*

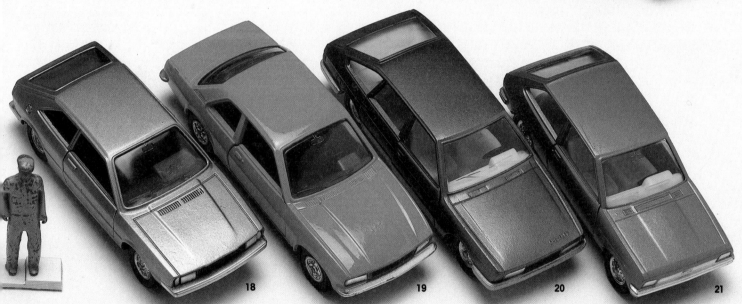

1970s. Finished in metallic green, this model features an opening bonnet and boot, clear plastic windows and a detailed interior. It is fitted with a plastic base. Length: 3·504in (89mm).

12 Peugeot 204 by Dinky Toys, Spain; SDT No 510, dating from the 1970s. Finished in ivory, this model has an opening bonnet, clear plastic windows and a detailed interior. As in (13) and (14), the body casting incorporates detail of a sun-roof. It has a metal base. See also *Inset, above right.* Length: 3·5625in (90mm).

13 Peugeot 304 by Dinky Toys, Spain; SDT No 1428, dating from the 1970s. Finished in metallic light green, this model has headlights and flashers with plastic lenses,

opening doors, clear plastic windows and a detailed interior. It is fitted with a plastic base. Length: 3·74in (95mm).

14 Peugeot 504 by Dinky Toys, Spain; SDT No 1452, dating from the 1970s. Finished in metallic gold, this model features an opening bonnet and boot, tinted plastic windows and a detailed interior. It is fitted with a metal base. Length: 4·134in (105mm).

15 Renault 12 by Dinky Toys, Spain; SDT No 1424, dating from the 1970s. Finished in yellow, this model has tinted plastic windows and a detailed interior. It is fitted with a plastic base. Length: 3·898in (99mm).

16 Renault R16 by Dinky Toys, Spain, SDT No 537, dating from the 1970s. Finished in silver, this

model features an opening bonnet, doors and hatchback, and a detailed interior with adjustable seats. This model is fitted with a metal base. Length: 3·819in (97mm).

17 Renault R16 TX by Dinky Toys, Spain; SDT No 538, dating from the 1970s. Finished in metallic plum, this model features an opening bonnet, doors and hatchback, and a detailed interior with adjustable seats. Its only major difference from the very similar model at (16) is in the design of the headlights. It has a metal base. Length: 3·819in (97mm).

18 Renault 14 by Dinky Toys, Spain; SDT No 1540, dating from the 1970s. Finished in metallic light green, this model has opening doors and a detailed interior. Its base is made of plastic.

Length: 3·622in (92mm).

19 Opel Ascona by Dinky Toys, Spain; SDT No 1543, dating from the 1970s. Finished in orange-yellow, this model features opening doors and a detailed interior. Its base is metal. Length: 3·898in (99mm).

20 Chrysler 1308 GT (Alpine) by Dinky Toys, Spain; SDT No 1542, dating from the 1970s. Finished in metallic turquoise, this model is fitted with opening doors and a detailed interior. Note the cast marque name on the bonnet. This model is fitted with a plastic base. Length: 3·74in (95mm).

21 Ford Fiesta by Dinky Toys, Spain; SDT No 1541, dating from the 1970s. Finished in metallic blue, this model has opening doors and a detailed interior. Its base is plastic. Length: 3·189in (81mm).

1 2 3 4

9 10 11

16 17 18

1 Iso Rivolta by Politoys, Italy;
maker's reference number (MRN)
515, dating from the 1960s. Finished
in metallic grey, this has an opening
bonnet, doors and boot, and a
detailed moulded interior (left-hand
drive) with folding seats. Note the
model's round, plated headlights.
Length: 4·3125in (110mm).
2 Lancia Flavia Coupé by Mercury,
Italy; MRN 32, dating from the
1960s. Finished in metallic
greenish-gold, this model features
an opening bonnet, doors and boot;
jewelled dual headlights and fog-
lamps; plated front and rear
bumpers; and a detailed moulded
plastic interior (left-hand drive).
Length: 4·134in (105mm).
3 Ferrari 250 GT 2+2 by Solido,
France, dating from the 1960s-70s.
Finished in red, it has opening

doors, a detailed interior and rather
crudely-rendered headlights.
Length: 4·134in (105mm).
4 Ferrari 250 GT Berlinetta by
Politoys, Italy; MRN 504, dating
from the 1960s. Finished in
metallic blue, this model features
an opening bonnet, doors and boot,
and a detailed interior. A
suspension system is fitted, and
its diecast base incorporates
details of transmission and exhaust.
Length: 4·016in (102mm).
5 Ferrari 330 GTC by Politoys, Italy;
MRN N652, dating from the
1960s. Finished in silver, this model
features opening doors and a
detailed interior (left-hand drive).
The body casting incorporates
side vents and a marque badge
on the bonnet. It has a diecast
base which incorporates details

of transmission and exhaust.
Length: 4·016in (102mm).
6 Ferrari 275 GTB by Dinky Toys,
Spain; MRN 506, dating from the
1960s. Finished in yellow, this
model features opening bonnet,
doors and boot; plated front and
rear bumpers; clear plastic windows
with a windscreen incorporating
wipers; headlights with clear
plastic lenses; and a detailed
interior. Length: 3·898in (99mm).
7 Ferrari 250 GT by Dinky Toys,
Spain; MRN 515, dating from the
1960s. Finished in metallic blue,
this model features an opening
bonnet and boot and a detailed
interior (right-hand drive). A
suspension system is fitted.
Length: 4·252in (108mm).
8 Ferrari 250 LM by Mercury,
Italy; dating from the 1960s.

Finished in red, with applied
badges and a white trim strip,
this model has opening doors, a
detailed moulded interior (right-
hand drive) and a lift-off cover
over the rear engine compartment.
Length: 3·74in (95mm).
9 Alfa Romeo 2600 by Solido,
France; MRN 125, dated (on base)
March 1963. Finished in metallic
gold, this has opening doors and
a detailed interior (left-hand
drive). Length: 4·134in (105mm).
10 Alfa Romeo Giulia TZ by
Politoys, Italy; MRN 516, dating
from the 1960s. Finished in red,
this model features plated wing
mirrors, opening doors, and a
detailed interior (left-hand drive)
which includes folding seats.
Length: 3·74in (95mm).
11 Alfa Romeo Giulia SS by

5

6

7

8

12

13

14

15

19

20

21

Politoys, Italy; MRN 506, dating from the 1960s. Finished in gold, this model has opening doors and boot and a detailed interior (left-hand drive) with folding seats. Length: 3·898in (99mm).

12 Alfa Romeo 1900 Super Sprint by Dinky Toys, Great Britain; Dinky Toys Reference Number (DT No) 185, first issued in January 1961 and available until 1963. Appearing only in yellow or red finish, this model features a moulded plastic interior (left-hand drive) and a suspension system incorporating "fingertip steering". It is now an item of limited availability. Length: 4·016in (102mm).

13 Lamborghini Bertone Espada by Politoys, Italy; MRN 587, dating from the 1960s. Finished in green, this model features opening bonnet,

doors and boot and a detailed interior (left-hand drive). It is fitted with plastic speedwheels. Length: 4·252in (108mm).

14 Lamborghini 350 GT by Politoys, Italy; MRN 539, dating from the 1960s. Finished in silver, this has opening bonnet, doors and boot, and a detailed interior (left-hand drive) with folding seats. Length: 4·016in (102mm).

15 Lamborghini Islero by Politoys, Italy; MRN 558, dating from the 1960s. Finished in gold, this model features a bonnet that opens to show a detailed engine; flip-up headlights; opening doors and a detailed interior (left-hand drive). Length: 4·134in (105mm).

16 Porsche 356A Coupé by Dinky Toys, Great Britain; DT No 182, first issued in September 1958

and available until 1966. Appearing in blue or cream finish only, it has clear plastic windows but no interior detail. It is fitted with metal wheels with detachable rubber tyres; its tinplate base is stamped with the maker's name, the number "182" and "Porsche 356A". Length: 3·504in (89mm).

17 Porsche 912 by Politoys, Italy; MRN 527, dating from the 1960s. Finished in silver, this has an opening bonnet, doors and boot, a detailed interior (left-hand drive), and a diecast base with suspension. Length: 3·74in (95mm).

18 Ghibli Maserati Ghia by Politoys, Italy; MRN 591, dating from the 1960s. Finished in yellow with a blue-and-white trim strip, it has opening doors and a detailed interior (left-hand drive). It is

fitted with plastic speedwheels. Length: 3·898in (99mm).

19 Maserati 3500 GT by Politoys, Italy; MRN 50, dating from the 1960s. Finished in blue, it has an opening bonnet, doors and boot, and a detailed interior (left-hand drive) with folding seats. Length: 4·252in (108mm).

20 Maserati Indy by Solido, France; MRN 185, dated (on base) February 1971. Finished in gold, it has opening doors and boot, a detailed interior (left-hand drive) and a plastic base. Length: 4·252in (108mm).

21 Maserati Coupé by Politoys, Italy; MRN 119, dating from the 1960s. Finished in red, it has an opening bonnet and doors, a detailed interior (left-hand drive), and a boot with a clear plastic cover. Length: 4·134in (105mm).

1
2
3
8
9
10
14
15
16

1 Lamborghini Urraco by Mebetoys, Italy; maker's reference number (MRN) A47, dating from c1970. Finished in yellow, this model features opening boot, bonnet and doors, a detailed moulded interior, and a suspension system. It is fitted with speedwheels. Length: 3·875in (98mm).
2 Toyota 2000GT by Mebetoys, Italy; MRN A29, dating from c1968. Finished in blue, this model shares the special features detailed at (1), although it is not fitted with speedwheels. Length: 3·75in (95mm).
3 Maserati Bora by Mebetoys, Italy; MRN 8554, dating from c1975. Finished in green, this model has the same features as (1), except that its base is plastic and no suspension is fitted. Length: 3·625in (92mm).

4 Ferrari 365 GTC-4 by Mebetoys, Italy; MRN A50, dating from c1970. Finished in blue and with the same features as (1), this model is shown with its bonnet raised to display its detailed engine. Length: 4·125in (105mm).
5 Porsche 924 by Schuco, West Germany; MRN 301628, dating from c1975. Finished in red, this model features an opening bonnet (with engine detail), boot and doors, and a detailed moulded interior. It has a suspension system and is fitted with speedwheels. Length: 3·875in (98mm).
6 Mercedes 350SE by Schuco, West Germany; MRN 301612, dating from c1978. Finished in blue, this model has opening doors (front only); otherwise it shares all the features detailed for the model at

(5). Length: 4·5in (114mm).
7 BMW 630CS by Schuco, West Germany; MRN 301629, dating from the late 1970s. Finished in chocolate, this model has all the features detailed for the car at (5). Length: 4·25in (108mm).
9 Fiat Abarth 2000 Pininfarina by

Dinky Toys, France; French Dinky Toys Reference Number (FDT No) 1430, dating from 1970. Finished in orange, it has an opening boot (showing engine detail) and a detailed moulded plastic interior. It is fitted with speedwheels. Length: 3·5in (89mm).
10 Porsche Carrera 6 by Dinky Toys, France; FDT No 503, dating from 1967. Finished in white, with red bonnet and chassis trim, this model features opening gull-wing doors and a boot that lifts to show a detailed engine. Length: 3·75in (95mm).
11 Matra Sports M530 by Dinky Toys, France; FDT No 1403, dating from 1967. Finished in orange, this model features opening doors and bonnet and a detailed moulded interior. Most notable, however,

8 Mercedes Benz C111 by Dinky Toys, Great Britain; Dinky Toys Reference Number (DT No) 224, first issued in 1970 and available until 1973. Produced in metallic dark red finish or, as seen at (14), in white, this model features opening gull-wing doors, opening boot (showing engine detail), and a detailed moulded interior (left-hand drive). It has a suspension system and is fitted with speedwheels. This is a common item. Length: 4·016in (102mm).

4 5 6 7

11 12 13

17 18 19

are its flip-up headlights (shown here in the retracted position) and lift-off roof panels (one is shown removed, beside the model). Length: 3·75in (95mm).

12 Peugeot 504 by Dinky Toys, France; FDT No 1415, dating from 1969. Finished in blue, this has opening doors back and front, windows all round, opening bonnet (showing engine detail) and boot, and a detailed moulded interior. Length: 4·06in (103mm).

13 Opel Rekord 1900 Coupé by Dinky Toys, France; FDT No 1405, dating from 1968. Finished in blue, this model features opening doors and bonnet (showing engine detail), a detailed moulded interior with tilting seats. It is fitted with a suspension system. Length: 4·21in (107mm).

14 Mercedes Benz C111; a colour variant of the model by Dinky Toys, Great Britain, fully noted at (8).

15 Dino Ferrari by Dinky Toys, Great Britain; DT No 216, first issued in 1967 and available until 1974. Seen here in blue rally finish, with the race number "20" (note also the number plate, and the Ferrari badge on the front wing), this model was also made in red finish. The casting incorporates an air vent in the bonnet, and the model features opening doors and boot and a detailed interior (right-hand drive). It is fitted with speedwheels. Although not at all scarce, this may prove a little harder to find than some of the later British Dinky models. Length: 3·858in (98mm).

16 Ferrari P5 by Dinky Toys, Great Britain; DT No 220, first issued in 1970 and available until 1974. Produced only with red body finish, this model features opening gull-wing doors, windows, a detailed moulded interior (right-hand drive), and a detailed rear-mounted engine compartment with spare wheel. It is fitted with speed-wheels. This is a fairly common item. Length: 3·78in (96mm).

17 Volvo 1800 S by Dinky Toys, Great Britain; DT No 116, first issued in 1966 and available until 1971. Produced in red finish only, this model features opening doors, bonnet and boot, a detailed moulded interior (left-hand drive) with tilting seats, jewelled headlights, and a suspension system. It is an item of limited availability.

Length: 4·134in (105mm).

18 Volkswagen 1300 Sedan by Dinky Toys, Great Britain; DT No 129, first issued in 1968 and available until 1974. Produced only in blue, this model features opening doors, bonnet and boot, a detailed interior (left-hand drive) with tilting seats, and jewelled headlights. It has a suspension system and speedwheels. A limited item. Length: 3·937in (100mm).

19 Monteverdi 375L by Dinky Toys, Great Britain; DT No 190, first issued in 1971 and available until 1973. Produced only in red, this model features opening doors and boot and a detailed interior (left-hand drive). Note the plated wing-mirrors. It is fitted with speedwheels. This is a common item. Length: 4·567in (116mm).

1

2

3

6

7

8

12

13

14

1 Mercedes Benz Geländewagen 240GD/230G/300GD/280GE by Cursor Modell, West Germany; maker's reference number (MRN) 679. Like the other West German models of modern and current vehicles shown on this spread, this model is intended for marketing in the show-rooms where the real cars are displayed—an effective promotional device used as early as the 1920s by Citroën of France. Finished in white with a black plastic canopy, this model of a utility vehicle features opening doors and a detailed plastic interior with folding seats. Like all the other models shown on this spread, it is fitted with plastic windows. It has plastic wheels fitted with rubber trackgrip tyres. Length: 4·724in (120mm).

2 Mercedes Benz 380SEC/500SEC Coupé by N.Z.G. Modell, West Germany; MRN 226, made to a scale of 1:35. Finished in red, this model features opening doors, bonnet and boot, and headlights with plastic lenses. Note the "Mercedes Benz" numberplate on this car and on that shown at (3). Its underside has a detailed chassis and exhaust system and its plastic wheels are fitted with treaded rubber tyres. Length: 5·512in (140mm).

3 Mercedes Benz 240TD/300TD/230T/250T/280TE Estate Car by Conrad Modell, West Germany; MRN 3065-3060, made to a scale of 1:35. This model features opening bonnet, front doors and tailgate. Its headlights and indicators have plastic lenses and it has a detailed chassis and exhaust.
Length: 5·315in (135mm).

4 Mercedes Benz 190/190E Saloon by Conrad Modell, West Germany; MRN 1182. Finished in pale grey, this model features opening doors, bonnet and boot, a detailed interior, and chassis and exhaust detail on its underside. It is fitted with treaded rubber tyres. Length: 4·921in (125mm).

5 Mercedes Benz 280S/SE/SEL by N.Z.G. Modell, West Germany; MRN 200. This photograph of the model provides an excellent display of its major features: opening doors, bonnet and boot, and plastic-lensed headlights, indicators and rearlights. It also has a detailed chassis and exhaust system. Length: 5·512in (140mm).

6 Volkswagen Passat GLS by Conrad Modell, West Germany; MRN 1010, made to a scale of 1:43. This model features opening doors, bonnet and tailgate and is fitted with chromed headlights. It has a detailed chassis and exhaust system. Length: 4·055in (103mm).

7 Volkswagen Passat Variant GLS by Conrad Modell, West Germany; MRN 1011. Finished in dark blue, this model features opening doors, bonnet and boot and chromed headlights. It has a detailed chassis and exhaust system. Length: 4·134in (105mm).

8 Volkswagen Scirocco GLI by Conrad Modell, West Germany; MRN 1013. Finished in metallic bronze, this model has opening doors, bonnet and tailgate and is fitted with chromed headlights. Length: 3·74in (95mm).

9 Volkswagen Santana GL by Conrad Modell, West Germany; MRN 1015. Finished in red, this model features opening bonnet, doors and tailgate, chromed headlights and a detailed underside. Length: 4·21in (107mm).

10 Toyota Celica LB 2000GT by Tomica, Japan; "Tomica Dandy" Series Number 021. Finished in black, this model has plastic windows that incorporate details of a rear-view mirror and windscreen wipers, opening doors and tailgate, and a detailed plastic interior. It is fitted with plastic bumpers and has plastic lenses over its rearlights. Length: 4·134in (105mm).

11 Mazda Savanna RL7 by Tomica, Japan; "Tomica Dandy" Series Number 008. The major feature of this model, which is finished in red, is its "pop-up" headlights,

controlled by a lever within the detailed interior. Its plastic windows incorporate details of a rear-view mirror and windscreen wipers. It has opening doors and is fitted with plastic bumpers; plastic lenses cover its rear-lights. Length: 4·016in (102mm).

12 Opel Ascona by Gama, West Germany; MRN 1141, made to a scale of 1:43. In silver and black finish, this model features opening doors and an opening tailgate. Length: 3·937in (100mm).

13-14 Audi Quattro by Conrad Modell, West Germany; MRN 1020, made to a scale of 1:43. Finished in metallic grey, (13) features opening bonnet, doors (bearing the Audi symbol) and boot, and has a detailed chassis. The version shown at (14) is in rally finish,

with "Audi" and "Castrol" on the bonnet and several other transfers. It is fitted with a rear-mounted plastic spoiler of a slightly different design to that on (13). Length: 4·055in (103mm).

15-17 B.M.W. M1 by Gama, West Germany; dating from around 1980. Three versions of this model by a maker currently noted for diecast cars in 1:43 scale are shown here. All three are fitted with opening doors and boot, well-detailed moulded interiors (left-hand drive), tinted plastic windscreens, and "pop-up" headlights with plastic lenses. The versions shown at (15) and (16) are in rally finish. The car at (15) is finished in black and silver, with the sponsors' names "Uher" and "Cassani" and other transfers, with the race

number "77". It has a cast metal skirt at the front end and a cast metal aerofoil at the rear. The example shown at (16) resembles it in all respects, but it is finished in red and white, with the name and logo of the sponsor, "BASF", and the race number "80". The example shown at (17) is in metallic silver finish, with no other markings, and lacks both the skirt and aerofoil of the rally-finished models. Diecast models of this kind, currently available from many European makers, are certainly most attractive and make fine display pieces; they are, however, probably best viewed as collectors' items for automobile enthusiasts rather than as toys in the true sense. Lengths (15-16): 4·21in (107mm); (17): 4·055in (103mm).

1 "General Lee" Car by Ertl, USA; dating from *c*1978 and made to a scale of approximately 1:24. Finished in orange, with the flag of the Confederate States applied on the roof, and the number "01" on the side, this model features a bonnet that opens to show a basically-detailed engine of plated plastic. The doors sand boot do not open. It has a tinted plastic windscreen, front quarterlights and rear window, a bright-plated plastic radiator and bumpers, and red plastic rear lights. The detailed interior of moulded plastic includes a roll-cage over the front seats. It is fitted with sculptured plastic wheels with fat, treaded "Good Year" rubber tyres. Its plastic base has moulded details of transmission, suspension and

exhaust. Length: 8·3125in (211mm).
2 Mercedes Benz 450SL by Polistil, Italy; dating from *c*1977 and made to a scale of 1:25. Finished in metallic blue, with a removable canopy (shown here in front of the model) of black plastic and a detailed black plastic interior (left-hand drive), this model has a bonnet that opens to show a fully-detailed engine of moulded plastic, opening doors and an opening boot. It has a plated plastic radiator, whip aerial and front and rear bumpers. A number plate, "SLM-P300", is fitted front and rear. It has a clear plastic windscreen and side windows, the latter shown in the half-down position. The plated plastic wheels are fitted with plastic tyres and the black plastic base bears

moulded details, including a bright-plated sump pan and exhaust system. Length: 7in (178mm).
3 Ford Capri by Dinky Toys, Great Britain; Dinky Toys Reference Number (DT No) 2162, first issued in 1974 and available until 1976. Two other versions of this large-scale model were issued at the same time: Ford Capri Rally Car, "Shell", DT No 2214; Ford Capri Police Car, DT No 2253. Finished in metallic blue with a black roof, this model has a bonnet (bearing the cast word "Ford") that opens to show a chromed plastic engine. It has opening front doors and an opening boot that bears the cast words "Ford" and "GXL". The front and rear bumpers and headlights are of chromed plastic; the rear lights are coloured plastic. It is fitted

with clear plastic windows (note the black plastic windscreen wipers) and has a detailed interior (right-hand drive) that includes folding seats. A number plate, "BTN 76", is fitted at the rear. The sculptured metal wheels are fitted with treaded plastic tyres, and the metal base plate has applied plastic details of transmission and exhaust. All three versions of this model are fairly common. Length: 6·89in (175mm).
4 B.M.W. 525 Berlina by Polistil, Italy; dating from *c*1975 and made to a scale of 1:25. Finished in metallic blue, this has an opening bonnet, showing an engine of plated plastic; opening front doors with plated plastic handles; and an opening boot. It has plated plastic front and rear bumpers and

headlights and red plastic rear-lights. The detailed interior includes a plated plastic steering wheel (left-hand drive) and gear lever. A number plate, "M1 W52107", is fitted front and rear. It has sculptured metal wheels with treaded plastic tyres and a plastic base with full moulded details. Length: 7·0625in (179mm).

5 Volkswagen by Polistil, Itay; dating from c1975 and made to a scale of 1:25. Finished in metallic blue, the model features a removable black plastic canopy and an opening bonnet. The front and rear bumpers, hood trim strip, whip aerial and windscreen wipers are black plastic; it has clear plastic headlights and red plastic rearlights. The moulded plastic interior includes folding seats

and a plated plastic steering wheel and gear lever. A number plate, "M1-V3 4824", is fitted at the rear. It has sculptured plastic wheels with treaded plastic tyres and a well-detailed plated plastic base. Length: 6·625in (168mm).

6 Porsche 930 Turbo by "G", Japan; dating from c1975 and made to a scale of 1:28. Finished in red with black trim, it has opening doors and a rear engine compartment, with spoiler, that opens to show a moulded plastic engine. The detailed interior (left-hand drive) is diecast and has tipping seats. The number plate, "IN-NA 44", is fitted front and rear. The sculptured metal wheels are fitted with fat, treaded rubber "Good Year" tyres. The metal base carries plated plastic details of the

suspension, sump and exhaust. Length: 6·125in (156mm).

7-9 Opel Ascona 400 Rally Car by Durago, Italy; dating from c1980 and made to a scale of 1:24. Three versions are shown. At (7), the model is finished in white, with a wealth of applied badges and trim strips and the number "2". The bonnet, edged with raised trim strips of black plastic, opens to show a plated plastic engine. The doors open on a moulded plastic interior (left-hand drive) with a plated plastic roll-cage at the rear. The boot, with spoiler, opens to show reserve petrol tanks of moulded plastic. It has a black plastic radiator with clear plastic headlights and orange plastic flashers, plated plastic foglights, and a rearlight assembly of

coloured plastic. A number plate, "M1-14292M", is fitted at the rear. The sculptured plastic wheels are fitted with fat plastic tyres; the front wheels are steerable. The plastic base has plated plastic details of transmission and exhaust, with twin pipes protruding at the rear. The car at (8), finished in metallic blue with a similar wealth of applied detail, differs from (7) in having no roll-cage, a different number plate ("CG-CJ 649"), and a base with moulded details that include a plated petrol tank. The car at (9), finished in red, has a base like that of (8), but features a roll-cage and has plastic spotlights fitted to the radiator. It bears the same rear number plate, "M1-14292M" as the car shown at (7). Length: 7·125in (181mm).

1 Rolls Royce Camargue by Durago, Italy; maker's reference number (MRN) 3001, dating from c1978 and made to a scale of 1:22. Finished in metallic grey, this large model features an opening bonnet, showing a detailed engine (complete with hoses of black plastic) of bright-plated moulded plastic, opening doors and an opening boot. The detailed interior (right-hand drive) includes folding seats and a simulated walnut dashboard with bright-plated instruments. A number plate, "PXC 162R", is fitted front and rear. It has clear plastic windows (the windscreen incorporating raised details of mirror and wind-screen wipers), plated plastic headlights and coloured plastic sidelights and flashers. The plated

radiator incorporates the famous Rolls Royce mascot. The metal wheels are fitted with plastic "Avon" tyres and it has a plastic base with moulded details of transmission and exhaust systems Length: 9·375in (238mm).
2 1912 Rolls Royce Silver Ghost by Corgi Toys, Great Britain; "Corgi Classics" Series Number 9041, issued in 1966 and available until 1970. Appearing in silver and black finish only, this model has a gilt metal roof rack (with spare tyre), tool box and spoked wheels (with treaded plastic tyres), metal radiator (with mascot), jewelled headlights, plated plastic carriage lamps, clear plastic windows and a detailed interior (right-hand drive) of moulded plastic. It has a cast chassis

incorporating full transmission details and a plastic exhaust system. Like all models in this series, it is increasingly hard to find. Length: 4·646in (118mm).
3-4 Rolls Royce Silver Shadow II by Durago, Italy; MRN 0134, dating from c1975 and made to a scale of 1:24. Two versions are shown, differing only in colour finish, (3) being in metallic blue and (4) in metallic grey, and in number plates: "SAR 841T" on (3) and "HFM 600N" on (4). The model has an opening bonnet, showing a detailed moulded plastic engine; front doors that open on to a detailed interior (left-hand drive) with folding front seats; and an opening boot. The radiator and dual headlight surrounds are plated plastic; the inset bumpers are

black plastic. It is fitted with sculptured plastic wheels and has a plastic base with details that include a plated exhaust system. Length: 7in (178mm).
5 Rolls Royce Phantom V by Dinky Toys, Great Britain; DT No 152, first issued in 1967 and available until 1975. Made only in dark blue or metallic blue (later examples), this model has doors that open on to a detailed plastic interior that includes the plastic half-figure of a chauffeur (right-hand drive). The radiator and front and rear bumpers are plated; it has jewelled dual headlights but rather crudely-painted red rearlights. The metal wheels are fitted with removable rubber tyres and the black metal base has basic details of exhaust and transmission. Suspension is.

fitted. This model is quite common. Length: 5·55in (141mm).

6 Bentley T Series by Corgi Toys, Great Britain; MRN 274, available 1970-72. Made only in pinkish-red finish, it has an opening bonnet, showing a plated plastic engine; front doors opening on to a detailed interior with folding seats and applied dashboard detail; and an opening boot. It has jewelled dual headlights and a plated metal radiator and bumpers. Fitted with sculptured plastic "whizzwheels", it has a plain grey metal base. This is one of the less common models in the series. Length: 4·724in (120mm).

7 Rolls Royce Corniche by Corgi Toys, Great Britain; issued in 1979 and currently available. Appearing also in metallic maroon finish, it

features opening doors, bonnet and boot and a well-detailed interior. Common. Length: 5·67in (144mm).

8 Rolls Royce Silver Cloud III by Polistil, Italy; dating from c1975 and made to a scale of 1:30. Finished in metallic grey, this model features such refinements as plated plastic wing mirrors and radio aerial; a two-piece bonnet that opens in gull-wing fashion to show a moulded plastic engine; black plastic windscreen wipers; and front doors with exterior and interior cast handles and interior cast detail of map pockets. A number plate, "FKV 899M", is fitted front and rear. The plastic wheels, with bright metal discs, are fitted with treaded plastic tyres and the plastic base is fully detailed. Length: 7·1875in (183mm).

9 Rolls Royce Silver Wraith by Dinky Toys, Great Britain; DT No 150, issued in 1959 and available until 1966. Made only in grey-and-dark-grey, it has chromed metal bumpers, radiator and headlights, and clear plastic windows. The aluminium wheels are fitted with detachable rubber tyres. The base plate is tinplate and a suspension system is fitted. Its availability is limited. Length: 4·606in (117mm).

10, 12 and **13** Rolls Royce Phantom III (1939 Model) by Solido, France; dated (on base) November 1976 and made to a scale of 1:43. Three versions of this model are shown. At (10) is an open car, finished in cream-and-black, with a simulated folded soft-top. At (12) is a "Berlin", with a cast metal top extending over the rear seats

and a rear-mounted boot. At (13) is a model with a black plastic soft-top fitted with plated plastic bracers. All are well-detailed with plated plastic parts and having wing-mounted spare wheels (plated plastic with treaded plastic tyres) and black cast metal bases with plastic details. Length: 5·0625in (129mm).

11 Rolls Royce Camargue by Asahi, Japan; dating from c1980 and made to a scale of 1:43. Finished in metallic dark grey, it has a bonnet that opens to show a plated plastic engine; opening front doors and a detailed interior that includes folding seats; and an opening boot. It has metal wheels fitted with treaded rubber "Avon" tyres and a detailed cast metal chassis. Length: 4·875in (124mm).

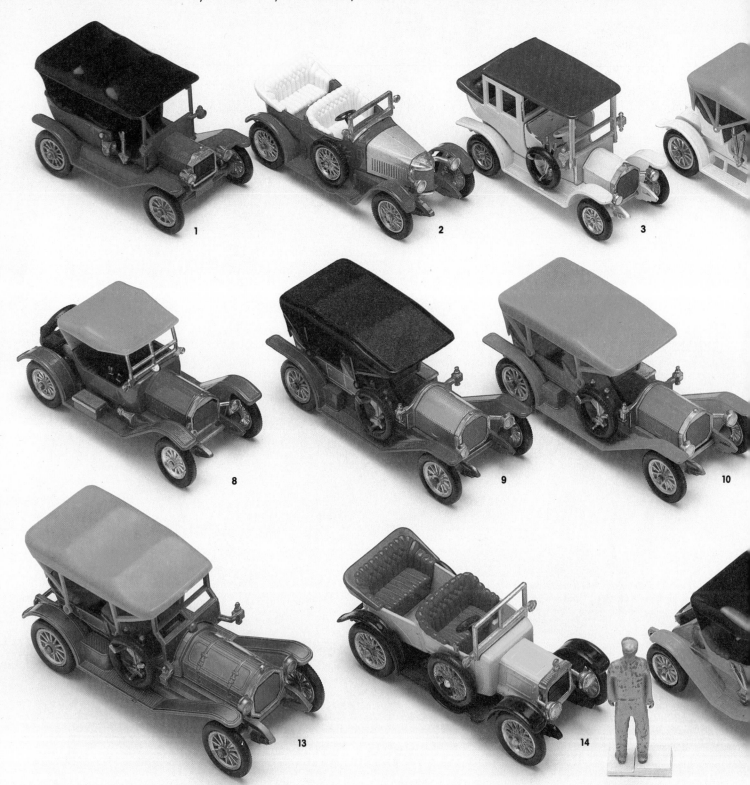

1911 Model "T" Ford by Lesney, Great Britain; Models of Yesteryear Number (MoY) Y-1 (2nd Issue)... **1**

1914 Prince Henry Vauxhall; MoY Y-2 (3rd Issue)... **2**

1910 Benz Limousine; MoY Y-3 (2nd Issue)... **3**

1914 Stutz; MoY Y-8 (3rd Issue)... **8**

1912 Simplex; MoY Y-9 (2nd Issue) (9) 1971 version... **9**

1912 Simplex (10) 1969 version... **10**

1907 Peugeot; MoY Y-5 (3rd Issue)... **13**

1912 Rolls Royce; MoY Y-7 (3rd Issue)... **14**

1 1911 Model "T" Ford by Lesney, Great Britain; Models of Yesteryear Number (MoY) Y-1 (2nd Issue), first issued, as shown, in 1964. A version with a white body and red roof was issued in 1974. In 1976, a limited edition of 1,000, with black body and black roof, was produced for the US market. This is rare and forgeries are known to exist; the other two versions are fairly common. Length: 2·992in (76mm).

2 1914 Prince Henry Vauxhall; MoY Y-2 (3rd Issue), first issued, as shown, in 1970; a variant with red seats is rare. A version with blue chassis and body and a silver bonnet was issued in 1974; a version with black chassis, red body and silver bonnet in 1979. All are common. Length: 3·5625in (90mm).

3 1910 Benz Limousine; MoY Y-3 (2nd Issue), first issued, as shown, in 1966. A version with pale green body and lemon roof was issued in 1968, and one with either pale green or dark metallic green body and black roof in 1970. The 1970 version is fairly common; others are limited. Length: 3·268in (83mm).

4 1909 Opel Coupé; MoY Y-4 (3rd Issue), first issued, as shown, with gold metal spoked wheels, in 1966. A version with orange body, black roof and silver plastic spoked wheels was issued in 1974. The later version is the harder to find. Length: 3·189in (81mm).

5 1907 Peugeot; MoY Y-5 (3rd Issue), first issued, as shown, with gold metal spoked wheels, in 1969. A version with bronze-orange body and roof, black seats and plastic spoked wheels was issued in 1974. Common. Length: 3·5625in (90mm).

6 1913 Cadillac; MoY Y-6 (3rd Issue), first issued, as shown, with gold metal spoked wheels, in 1967. A version with green body, black roof and silver plastic spoked wheels was issued in 1974. Both versions are fairly common. Length: 3·386in (86mm).

7 1912 Rolls Royce; MoY Y-7 (3rd Issue), first issued, as shown, with a red smooth roof and gold metal spoked wheels, in 1968. The subsequent versions were: (1969) silver body and grey smooth roof; (1970) silver body and grey ribbed roof; (1970, second change) silver body and red ribbed roof; (1974) gold body, red ribbed roof; silver plastic spoked wheels; (1979) yellow body, black ribbed roof, red plastic spoked wheels. The second 1970 version is rare; the 1968 and 1969 versions are limited; all others are fairly common. Length: 3·858in (98mm).

8 1914 Stutz; MoY Y-8 (3rd Issue), first issued, as shown, with gold metal spoked wheels, in 1969. A version with blue body, black roof and silver plastic spoked wheels was issued in 1974. Both are quite common. Length: 3·504in (89mm).

9-10 1912 Simplex; MoY Y-9 (2nd Issue), first issued in 1968. The versions shown here are: (9) 1971 version, with plastic spoked wheels; (10) 1969 version, with metal spoked wheels. Other versions are: (1968) yellow-green body, tan roof, red seats and gold metal spoked

wheels; (1974) red body, black roof, yellow seats, red plastic spoked wheels; (1979) black chassis, red body, yellow roof and seats, red plastic spoked wheels. The 1968 and 1969 versions are limited; the others are fairly common. Length: 3·78in (96mm).

11 1906 Rolls Royce "Silver Ghost"; MoY Y-10 (3rd Issue), first issued, as shown, with gold metal spoked wheels, in 1969. Further versions were: (1974) white body, black seats (also found with red seats), silver plastic spoked wheels; (1979) silver body, dark red seats, red plastic spoked wheels; (1979, second change) silver body, yellow seats, red plastic spoked wheels. The version shown is limited; the rest should not be too hard to find. Length: 3·622in (92mm).

12 1912 Packard Landaulet; MoY Y-11 (2nd Issue), issued in 1964. It is found with either gold or silver metal spoked wheels and a metal or plastic steering wheel. Common. Length: 3·15in (80mm).

13 1909 Thomas Flyabout; MoY Y-12 (2nd Issue), first issued, with blue body, tan roof, yellow seats and gold or silver metal spoked wheels, in 1967. The second version of 1967, shown here, differed in having dark red seats. The 1974 version had a red body, black roof, white seats and silver metal spoked wheels. Both the version shown and the 1974 version are common. Length: 3·898in (99mm).

14 1911 Daimler; MoY Y-13 (2nd Issue), first issued, with yellow body, black chassis, black seats and gold metal spoked wheels, in 1966. The 1967 version, shown here, differs in having red seats. Common. Length: 3·307in (84mm).

15 1911 Maxwell Roadster; MoY Y-14 (2nd Issue), issued in 1965. This model may be found with a black or tan roof and with gold or silver metal spoked wheels. It is fairly common. Length: 3·228in (82mm).

16 1930 Packard Victoria; MoY Y-15 (2nd Issue), first issued, as shown, in 1969. This version may be found with gold or silver metal spoked wheels. Other versions are: (1974) greenish-gold body, black roof and silver plastic spoked wheels (1979) black and red body, white roof, silver plastic bolt head wheels and whitewall tyres. The 1969 version is limited; the other versions are common. Length: 4·291in (109mm).

17 1904 Spyker; MoY Y-16 (1st Issue), first issued, as shown, in 1961. The version issued in 1968 has a darker yellow body. Both versions are limited. Length: 3·268in (83mm).

Inset (above centre): *The 1904 Spyker, Model of Yesteryear Number Y-16 (1st Issue), is shown here in chrome-plated form. Models found in this finish (and also in gold) were originally sold mounted on ashtrays, cigarette boxes and the like. They will be found to have mounting holes for this purpose in their base plates; similar holes may also be found on some other models which have otherwise conventional finishes.*

1

3

4

6

1 Firebird Racer (manufacturer's serial number TP.102) by Tomiyama, Japan, dating from c1958-59. This interesting tinplate representation of what is described on the box as an "Indianapolis special type" racing car has on either side an applied metal plate printed "Indianapolis 500" and has the number "1107" printed on its tail fin. The race number "3" is printed on a white applied metal plate at the front. With operating steering, it is powered by a battery housed in a trap on the underside. An on/off switch is situated towards the rear on the underside. When power is switched on, "engine noise" is produced, the engine compartment lights up under its red plastic cover, and the exhaust (on the side away from

the camera) sparks. The engine stops, then starts again, and as the car moves away the driver (with a pressed-tin torso and plastic head and limbs).signals with his pivoted right arm. The plastic wheels, with simulated knock-on hubcaps, are fitted with rubber tyres. A fairly scarce toy. Length: 14·5in (36·83cm).
2 Champion Racer 301 by "TM", Japan, dating from 1959. This large tinplate racing car is battery-powered (an identical car was made with friction-drive), with an on/off switch beneath the rear of the car near the battery compartment. When power is switched on and the car is moving, the plastic cylinders of the simulated V6 engine light up, as does the plastic housing of the exhaust system, with its

pressed-tin pipe. A pair of variable-steering wheels mounted on a turntable in the base cause the car to run an erratic course. Note the printed detail of louvres and air vents. The figure of the driver is tinplate, with a detachable rubber head, and the plastic, whitewalled wheels are fitted with rubber tyres. Length: 17·75in (45·085cm).
3 Corvair Bertone (manufacturer's serial number 4085) by Bandai, Tokyo, Japan, dating from 1966. This fine tinplate model of a luxury sports car is powered by two 1·5-volt batteries housed in a base trap: these transmit power to a pair of variable-steering wheels mounted in the base. The mechanism starts and stop intermittently: while the car is moving,

the headlights light up and "engine noise" is produced; when it stops, the headlights retract into the bonnet and the plastic canopy opens. The figure of the driver (left-hand drive) is plastic. The wheel are rubber and are fitted with rubber tyres and plastic hubcaps. Length: 12·5in (31·12cm).
4 JNF Racing Car (manufacturer's serial number 82) by JNF, West Germany, dating from c1957-58. This is a good-quality tinplate model of a Mercedes Type 196 racing car (note the Mercedes star on the bright metal radiator grille) and is friction-driven. The body pressing incorporates details of an eight-cylinder engine on the base; other details include pressed-tin exhausts, a plated rear-view mirror, a plastic

windscreen, and a printed cockpit. The pressed-tin steering wheel is operational and the metal wheels, with well-modelled bright metal discs, are fitted with rubber tyres. See also (7) on this spread. Length: 9·5in (24·13mm).

5 Ferrari Gear Shift Car (with the manufacturer's serial number 4183) by Bandai, Japan, dating from c1965. This fine battery-powered model has a tinplate body with plated bumpers, mascot, air vent, door handles and windscreen frame (with celluloid screen). The pressed-tin interior has printed upholstery. Powered by two 1·5-volt batteries housed in a trap on the underside, it features operating steering (left-hand drive), a working horn, "engine noise", and working head- and rear-lights. Its

most notable features are a working gear lever, giving high, low and neutral, and a further lever giving forward, reverse or stop. It has rubber tyres on well-modelled plastic wheels. A similar model by Bandai, the Cadillac Gear Shift Car, is shown at (1), on *pages 42-43*. Length: 11·125in (28·26cm).

6 MGA 1600 Hardtop by Sanshin, Japan, dating from c1958. This fairly simple tinplate model of a British sports car (although shown with left-hand drive) is clockwork-driven—the winding shaft is on the side away from the camera—and is steered by a simple bulb-and-tube acting on a single variable-steering wheel in the base. It has bright metal bumpers, radiator, bonnet and door handles; printed details include upholstery, a

simple dashboard, and transmission and suspension on the base. The rubber wheels are fitted with metal discs. Length: 7·125in (18·097cm).

7 JNF *Silberpfeil* (Silver Arrow) Car (manufacturer's serial number 78) by JNF, West Germany, dating from c1957-58. This streamlined version of a Mercedes Type 196 racing car—see also (4)—is clockwork-powered. It is a toy of good quality and features an operating steering wheel and handbrake, a detachable plastic windscreen, and a tinplate body pressing that incorporates louvres and pierced vents. The composition driver is detachable. The metal wheels are fitted with detachable metal hubcaps and rubber tyres. Length: 10·625in (26·987cm).

8 Racing Car by Joustra (Societé

d'Exploitation du Jouet Joustra), Strasbourg-Neudorf, France, dating from 1956; note the maker's trademark and "Made in France" stamped at the lower rear. This car, more "toy-like" in quality than most of the other examples shown here, has a simple streamlined body pressing with brightly-printed details. The wheels are exposed—although on a streamlined racing car they would normally be enclosed within the body shell—and are provided with detailed coil suspension of wire and pressed-tin. The metal wheels, with detachable hubcaps are fitted with rubber tyres. The figure of the driver is plastic, as is the windscreen. This is a friction-drive car, with no provision made for steering. Length: 11·125in (28·257cm).

1-3 Racing Car by Dinky Toys, Great Britain; Dinky Toys Reference Number (DT No) 23a. Three examples are shown of a very simple yet long-lived model that first appeared in April 1934. (Note that the colour finishes on the models shown appear to be non-original.) The various versions of this model, with their major identification points, are: (1934-35) orange-and-green body, four exhaust stubs and no driver—as (3); (1935-38) blue-and-white body, with driver and cast detail of six-branched exhaust system—as (1) and (2)—with raised ridge around racing number; (1938-40) red body with cream flash, no ridge around racing number; (1946-48) blue body with silver flash, cast-in driver, no race

number; (1949-52) red body with silver flash, race number "4" in black circle; (1953-54) silver body with red flash, number "4" in red circle. The 1934-35 version is rare; the versions issued between 1935 and 1948 are scarce; 1949-54 versions are of limited availability: a desirable item in any version. Length (all versions): 3·7in (94mm).

4 Mercedes Benz Racing Car ("Large Open Racing Car"); DT No 23c. This model was first issued in May 1936 and was available in red or blue, with the race number "2" in a yellow circle, until 1940. It was reissued, renamed "Large Open Racing Car", in 1947-50, appearing in silver or blue finish, as shown. The pre-War version is scarce;

the post-War version is limited. Length: 3·622in (92mm).

5 Auto Union Racing Car; DT No 23d. This was first issued in May 1936 and was available in red or blue, with various race numbers in white or yellow circles and with the diecast figure of a driver slotted in, until 1940. It was reissued in 1947-50, as shown, without a driver. The pre-War version is scarce; the post-War version is extremely limited. Length: 3·937mm (100mm).

6 Alpine F111 Racing Car by Solido, France; maker's reference number (MRN) 142, issued in July 1965. It is fitted with suspension and has an overalled plastic driver. Length: 3·307in (84mm).

7 Lola Climax V8 F1 (ie, Formula One) Racing Car by Solido,

France; MRN 135, issued in July 1964. It is fitted with suspension and has engine and exhaust detail; the figure of the driver is plastic. Length: 3·504in (89mm).

8 Ferrari V12 F1 by Solido, France; MRN 167, issued in June 1968. This model has no driver and is not fitted with suspension, but it has a detailed engine and exhaust system. See also (15). Length: 3·74in (95mm).

9 Matra Sports F2 (ie, Formula Two) Racing Car by Norev, France; MRN 601, dating from c1966. This model is fitted with suspension and has a detailed exhaust; the figure of the driver is plastic. Length: 3·7in (94mm).

10 Cooper Maserati Racing Car by Corgi Toys, Great Britain; MRN 156. First issued in 1967 and

available until 1969, it has a detailed engine and exhaust, a plastic driver and plated mirrors. Length: 3·5625in (90mm).

11 Matra V112 F1 by Dinky Toys, France; French Dinky Toys Reference Number (FDT No) 1417, dating from 1969. A fully-detailed model, fitted with suspension system. Length: 3·74in (95mm).

12 Lotus Climax Racing Car by Corgi Toys, Great Britain; MRN 155, issued in 1965-68. A well-detailed model, with plated rear-view mirror and exhaust system, fitted with suspension. Like the other Corgi models shown on this spread, it is fairly easy to find. Length: 3·5625in (90mm).

13 Surtees TS5 by Dinky Toys, France; FDT No 1433, dating from 1971. A well-detailed model with

suspension. Length: 3·7in (94mm).

14 Matra V8 F1 by Solido, France; MRN 173, issued in June 1969. The wealth of detail on this model includes a cast aerofoil at the rear. Length: 4·055in (103mm).

15 Ferrari V12 F1 by Solido, France; MRN 167, issued in June 1968. This is basically the same model as (8), but with the addition of an aero-foil and the figure of a driver. Length: 3·74in (95mm).

16 Lotus Climax Racing Car by Corgi Toys, Great Britain; MRN 158, issued in 1969-72. It differs from the earlier version shown at (12), most obviously in having an aerofoil. It is fitted with a suspension system and features driver-controlled steering; the driver is a plastic figure. Length: 3·504in (89mm).

17 Ferrari V12 F1 by Dinky Toys, France; FDT No 1422, dating from 1969. It features rather more detail that the model of the same car by Solido, shown at (15). Length: 3·7in (94mm).

18 Cooper Maserati by Corgi Toys, Great Britain; MRN 159, issued in 1969-72. Like (16), this model features driver-controlled steering; the driver is plastic and it is fitted with suspension. An earlier version (MRN 156, dating from 1967-69) was finished in blue with the race number "7"; see (10). Length: 3·5625in (90mm).

19-24 Cooper Norton Racing Car by Tekno, Denmark; MRN 812, dating from around 1958. This most attractive little model, with a plastic driver and detail of engine and exhaust, with suspension

fitted, is shown in the racing colours of France (19), Great Britain (20), Switzerland (21), Netherlands (22), the German Federal Republic (23), and Belgium (24). Length: 2·9375in (75mm).

25 Indianapolis S.T.P. Turbine Car by Faracars, France (made under licence from USA); MRN 101, dating from c1970. A solid and well-detailed model of good quality, this represents the first turbine-engined car (Pratt & Whitney STGB-62 550bhp turbine) to run at the famous "Indy" track in the USA, in 1967. Length: 3·504in (89mm).

26 Harvey Aluminium Indianapolis Special by Solido, France; MRN 138, issued in February 1965. This model is fitted with a suspension system and has a plastic driver. Length: 3·15in (80mm).

Diecast Racing Cars by European Makers, 1950s-1960s

1 Alta Racing Car by Scamold, Great Britain; maker's reference number (MRN) 105, dating from around 1950. Finished in silver, with a green cockpit, this model features a detailed cockpit and exhaust system and is fitted with treaded rubber tyres. Length: 4·37in (111mm).

2-3 Maserati Racing Car by Scamold, Great Britain; MRN 103, dating from c1950. Two versions are shown: (2) is finished in dark blue, with a lighter blue cockpit; (3) is finished in dark blue, with a silver radiator and brown cockpit. The major difference is that (3) is fitted with a spring motor; note the winding-shaft that protrudes at the base of the radiator. Note also that (2), like the other unpowered Scamold models shown here, has a clearly-visible aperture in the

body casting to accommodate a winding-shaft Both racing cars are fitted with treaded rubber tyres. Length: 4·252in (108mm).

4-6 E.R.A. Racing Car by Scamold, Great Britain; MRN 101, dating from around 1950. Three versions are shown: (4) is finished in light green, with a grey radiator and cockpit, and is not fitted with a motor; (5) is finished in dark green, with a blue radiator and cockpit, and is fitted with a spring motor; (6) is finished in yellow, with a black radiator bearing the race number "34", bonnet straps in black and blue cockpit, and, like the car at (4), is unpowered. All are fitted with treaded rubber tyres. Length: 4·37in (111mm).

7 Maserati Racing Car by Mercury, Italy; MRN 31, dating from 1960. Finished in red, with white treaded

rubber tyres, this simple model bears on its tail the race number "2". Length: 3·504in (89mm).

8 Cisitalia 1100 Racing Car by Mercury, Italy; MRN 37, dating from 1955, and finished in blue, with a silver radiator and brown cockpit. This model bears the race number "6" and has cast wheels fitted with detachable grey rubber treaded tyres. Length: 3·74in (95mm).

9 Maserati Grand Prix Racing Car by Mercury, Italy; MRN 34, dating from 1957. Finished in red, with a silver radiator and the race number "7", this model is fitted with detachable white treaded rubber tyres. Length: 4·252in (108mm).

10 S.V.A. Racing Car by Mercury, Italy; MRN 39, dating from 1955. Finished in green, with a silver radiator and the race number "6",

this racing car is fitted with detachable black treaded rubber tyres. Length: 3·504in (89mm).

11 Alfa Romeo Alfette 158 Racing Car by Mercury, Italy; MRN 35, dating from 1957. Finished in red, with a silver radiator but no race number, this model has detachable brown treaded rubber tyres. Length: 4·252in (108mm).

12 Mercedes Benz 1500 Racing Car by Mercury, Italy; MRN 40, dating from 1955. Finished in white, with a black-barred radiator, brown cockpit and the race number "3", this simple but nicely finished model is fitted with detachable grey rubber treaded tyres. Length: 4·17in (106mm).

13 Ferrari 1500 Racing Car by Mercury, Italy; MRN 36, dating from 1955. Finished in red, with a silver

radiator and the race number "5" in white, this model is fitted with detachable treaded rubber tyres. Length: 4·252in (108mm).

14 Cisitalia 1500 Grand Prix Racing Car by Mercury, Italy; MRN 38, dating from 1955. Finished in silver, with a black-barred radiator, black cockpit and black-outlined door panels, and without a race number, this racing car is fitted with detachable grey rubber treaded tyres. Length: 4·3125in (110mm).

15 Vanwall Formula One Racing Car by Solido, France; dating from the 1960s. Finished in dark green, with the applied name "Vanwall" and race number "9", this model features a clear plastic wraparound windscreen; a cockpit with the plastic figure of an overalled, helmeted driver; and, like the other Solido

models shown here, wheels that incorporate details of brake drums. Length: 4·016 (102mm).

16 Maserati 250 Racing Car by Solido, France; dating from the 1960s. Finished in yellow, with the race number "3", this model features a clear plastic windscreen, a cockpit with plastic driver, and a cast metal exhaust system at the side. Length: 3·74in (95mm).

17 Lola Climax V8 Formula One Racing Car by Solido, France; dating from the 1960s. Finished in dark blue, with a red-banded nose and the race number "2", this model features a cockpit with driver, bright-plated details of engine and exhaust pipes, and a detailed cast metal suspension system. Length: 3·504in (89mm).

18-19 Porsche F.11 Racing Car by

Solido, France; dating from the 1960s. Two versions are shown: (18) is finished in light green and bears the race number "10"; (19) is finished in silver, with a tri-colour trim strip, and bears the race number "3". The model has a body casting that incorporates the outline of an engine cover, and it features a clear plastic wraparound windscreen, a cockpit with the plastic figure of a driver, and rear exhaust details. Length: 3·268in (83mm).

20 Lotus Formula One Racing Car by Solido, France; MRN 118, dating from 1961. Made to a scale of 1:43, like all the Solido racing cars of the late 1950s-early 1960s shown on this spread, it is finished in dark green and bears the race number "3" on its nose. The cockpit, with an overalled and helmeted driver,

is protected by a full wraparound screen of clear plastic, and it has cast metal details of an exhaust system. Length: 3·071in (78mm).

21 Cooper 1·5-Litre Racing Car by Solido, France; MRN 116, dating from 1959. Finished in dark green, with the race number "3", this model features a cockpit with a driver protected by a wraparound screen, and a cast metal exhaust system. Length: 3·071in (78mm).

22 B.R.M. V8 Racing Car by Solido, France; MRN 131, dated (on base) February 1964. Finished in dark green, with the race number "3", this model has a clear plastic wraparound windscreen, a cockpit with driver, cast details of a roll-over bar behind the cockpit, and a cast metal exhaust system. Length: 3·386in (86mm).

1 B.R.M. Mark II Grand Prix Car by Crescent Toys, Great Britain; Crescent Toys Reference Number (CTN) 1285, issued in 1957. Crescent's series of eight racing cars and two sports racing cars—shown on this spread at (1-7) and (9-11)—probably includes this maker's most sought-after models. As in all Crescent racing cars, the figure of the overalled driver is cast as part of the base plate. Length: 3·858in (98mm).

2 Maserati 2·5-litre Grand Prix Car: CTN 1290, issued in 1957. Note that the example shown here has been repainted, with added detail on such features as the driver's helmet and the filler cap on the car's tail. Length: 3·898in (99mm).

3 "D" Type, Jaguar 3·5-litre Sports Racing Car; CTN 1292, issued in

1957. The example shown has been carefully repainted, with certain details highlighted, as at (2). Length: 3·74in (95mm).

4 Aston Martin D.B.3S 2·9-litre Sports Racing Car; CTN 1291, issued in 1957. This attractive model is finished in American racing colours. Length: 3·74in (95mm).

5 Mercedes-Benz 2·5-litre Grand Prix Car; CTN 1284, issued in 1957. Length: 4·17in (106mm).

6 Connaught 2-litre Grand Prix Car; CTN 1287, issued in 1957. Length: 3·858in (98mm).

7 Gordini 2·5-litre Grand Prix Car; CTN 1289, issued in 1957. This example has been repainted. Note that it has also been refitted with tyres of the kind used on the racing cars issued by Corgi Toys, Great Britain; compare with the

other Crescent cars shown here. Length: 3·346in (85mm).

8 Ferrari Racing Car by Dinky Toys, France; French Dinky Toys Reference Number 23j, issued in 1957. It is finished in red, the racing colours of Italy; note the similarity otherwise with the British-made version in the racing colours of Argentina, shown at (15). Length: 3·937in (100mm).

9 Ferrari 2·5-litre Grand Prix Car; CTN 1286, issued in 1957. Note that the example shown here has been repainted and that new transfer detail has been applied. Length: 3·937in (100mm).

10 Cooper Bristol 2-litre Grand Prix Car; CTN 1288, issued in 1957. Length: 3·307in (984mm).

11 Vanwall 2·5-litre Grand Prix Car; CTN 1293, issued in 1957.

This is the hardest model to find of the set of Crescent racing cars. Length: 4·055in (103mm).

12 H.W.M. Racing Car by Dinky Toys, Great Britain; Dinky Toys Reference Number (DT No) 23j, first issued in May 1953, renumbered 235 in 1954, and available until 1960. It appeared only in green with the race number "7" in yellow. As in the other Dinky racing cars shown on this spread, the figure of the driver and also the steering wheel are cast in. The model's tinplate base plate is stamped with the maker's name, "23J" ("235" on later examples) and "H.W.M." It is of limited availability, examples numbered "23J" being more highly valued by collectors. Length: 3·989in (99mm).

13 Maserati Racing Car; DT No 23n, first issued in June 1953, renumbered 231 in 1954, and available until 1964. Appearing only in red with a white flash (Swiss racing colours), with the number "9" in white, it has a tinplate base that bears the maker's name, "23N" ("231" later) and "Maserati". Its availability is as noted for the item at (12). Length: 3·7in (94mm).

14 Talbot-Lago Racing Car; DT No 23k, first issued in September 1953, renumbered 230 in 1954, and available until 1964. Appearing only in blue with the number "4" in yellow, it has a tinplate base that bears the maker's name, "23K" ("230" later) and "Talbot Lago". As with (13), (15), (16) and (17), earlier versions have

ridged diecast wheels, while later examples (like the ones shown on this spread), dating from about the last two years of manufacture, may have plastic wheels; rubber tyres being fitted in all cases. Availability of this model is as (12). Length: 4·055in (103mm).

15 Ferrari Racing Car; DT No 23h, issued in April 1953, renumbered 234 in 1954, and available until 1964. It appeared only in blue, but earlier versions have an all-yellow nose whereas later examples, like that shown here, have a yellow triangle. All bear the race number "5" in yellow. Its tinplate base bears the maker's name, "23H" ("234" later) and "Ferrari". Availability as (12). Length: 3·976in (101mm).

16 Alfa-Romeo Racing Car; DT No 23f, issued in August 1952, renum-

bered 232 in 1954, and available until 1964. It appeared only in red with the white number "8". Its tinplate base bears the maker's name, "23F" ("232" later) and "Alfa-Romeo". Availability as (12). Length: 3·937in (100mm).

17 Cooper-Bristol Racing Car; DT No 23g, first issued in March 1953, renumbered 233 in 1954, and available until 1964. It appeared only in green with the race number "6" in white. Its tinplate base bears the maker's name, "23G" ("233" later) and "Cooper-Bristol". Availability as (12). It is worth noting that the six Dinky racing cars shown here at (12-17) were issued as Gift Set Number 4, available from 1953 until 1955 and now scarce and eagerly sought. Length: 3·504in (89mm).

Inset (top right): *Racer by Dinky Toys, Great Britain; Dinky Toys Reference Number 35b. Three versions of this long-lived, if diminutive, model are shown. (Left) As issued in 1939-40, with silver body, brown driver, red grille, and solid black rubber wheels: length: 2·323in (59mm). (Centre) As first issued in 1936-39, with red body, silver grille, no driver, and solid black (also found with white) rubber wheels; length: 2·402in (61mm). (Right) As issued in 1954-57, when the model was renamed Midget Racer and renumbered 200. Red or silver versions are recorded: this example finished in green appears to be a variant. Length: 2·244in (57mm). All versions are of fairly limited availability.*

1 Aston Martin DB3 (thus catalogued; in fact, an Aston Martin DB 2-4 Mk III) by Spot On (Tri-ang); Lines Bros Ltd), Great Britain; maker's reference number (MRN) 113, issued in 1960. Finished in metallic green, and appearing also in other colours, this has clear plastic windows and a detailed interior. Like all the Spot On cars shown here, it is made to a scale of 1:42, and, like all save (9), it has a metal chassis and is fitted with treaded rubber tyres. Like most Spot On models, it is now of scarce availability. Length: 4·094in (104mm).

2 Jaguar XKSS by Spot On; MRN 107, issued in 1960. Appearing only in red or green, this is fitted with front and rear number plates and has a clear plastic windscreen, interior detail, and a body casting that

incorporates a folded hood. It is one of the less common Spot On cars. Length: 3·583in (91mm).

3 Daimler SP250 Dart by Spot On; MRN 215, issued in 1962. Finished in yellow, and appearing also in other colours, this has a bright-plated radiator. Like (2), it may be hard to find. Length: 3·819in (97mm).

4 Sunbeam Alpine Convertible by Spot On; MRN 191, issued in 1963: a hard-top version was issued under the same number in the same year. Finished in blue, and appearing also in other colours, this has plated bumpers, radiator and headlight surrounds. The convertible may be slightly easier to find than the hardtop. Length: 3·74in (95mm).

5 M.G.A. Sports Car by Spot On; MRN 104, issued in 1959. Finished in red, and appearing also in white

or blue, this has a particularly well-detailed interior. It is one of the scarcer items in the Spot On range. Length: 3·74in (95mm).

6 M.G. Midget Mk II by Spot On; MRN 281, issued in 1966. Finished in white, this features plated parts and a detailed interior with a cast driver. Length: 3·268in (83mm).

7-8 M.G. Sports Car by Dinky Toys, Great Britain; Dinky Toys Reference Number (DT No) 35c. This model was first issued in 1936, remaining available until 1940: pre-War versions, in red, green or blue finish, have solid white rubber wheels. It was reissued, in red (7) or green (8), with solid black rubber wheels, in 1946-48. Both pre- and post-War versions are now hard to find. Length: 2·047in (52mm).

9 M.G. PB Midget (1935 Model) by

Spot On; MRN 729, issued in 1965. Appearing only in red-and-black finish, this model has a plastic chassis. It features plated parts and a detailed interior, and has cast-in spoked wheels. Another scarce item. Length: 3·11in (79mm).

10 M.G. TD Midget by Tekno, Denmark; dating from the early 1950s. Finished in red, with cream and pink trim, this model has a detailed interior with a bright-plated steering wheel (left-hand drive), and like the MG at (9), a rear-mounted spare wheel. Length: 3·465in (88mm).

11 M.G.C. GT by Corgi Toys, Great Britain; MRN 378, issued in 1970 and available until 1972. Appearing only in red-and-black finish, this model features jewelled headlights, opening doors and hatchback (with tool kit, as shown) tinted plastic

5

6

7   8

9

10

15   16   17   18

23   24   25

windows and a detailed interior. It is fitted with plastic "whizz-wheels". Length: 3·5625in (90mm).

12 M.G.B. GT by Corgi Toys; MRN 327, issued in 1967 and available until 1968. Appearing only in red, this model has jewelled headlights, an opening bonnet, doors and hatch-back (including tool kit), and a detailed interior. Like (11), it will not be particularly easy to find. Length: 3·5625in (90mm).

13 Jaguar XK120 by Tekno, Denmark; dating from the early 1950s. This quite elegant little model has twin aero-screens of clear plastic and a detailed interior (left-hand drive). Length: 3·386in (86mm).

14 Austin Healey 100 (Touring Finish) by Dinky Toys, Great Britain; DT No 103, first issued in 1957 and available until 1960. Appearing only

in red and cream finish, this has a cast driver, a tinplate base and detachable rubber tyres. Limited. Length: 3·425in (87mm).

15 Austin Healey 100-4 by Corgi Toys; MRN 300, issued in 1956 and available until 1963. Compare this car with the Dinky Toys model at (14). This has a cast-in steering wheel, but no driver. It is of limited availability. Length: 3·386in (86mm).

16 Austin Healey Sprite Mark II by Dinky Toys, Great Britain; DT No 112, issued in November 1961 and available until 1966. Appearing only in red, this model is fitted with suspension and a "fingertip steering" system. Its availability is limited. Length: 3·071in (78mm).

17 M.G.A. Coupé by Tekno, Denmark; dating from the late 1950s. Finished in light blue, it has a detailed

moulded interior (left-hand drive). Length: 3·5625in (90mm).

18 Jaguar "E" Type by Corgi Toys; MRN 374, issued in 1970 and available until 1976. Finished in dark blue, this has plated parts, a detailed interior and "whizz-wheels". Length: 4·252in (108mm).

19-20 Vanwall Racing Car by Corgi Toys; MRN 150/150S. No 150, without driver or suspension, was available 1957-61; No 150S, with driver and suspension, was available 1961-65. It is now a limited item. Length: 3·583in (91mm).

21 B.R.M. Racing Car by Corgi Toys; MRN 152/152S. No 152, without suspension, was available 1958-61; No 152S, with suspension, was available 1961-65. Neither is common. Length: 3·583in (91mm).

22 Mercedes Benz 196 Grand Prix

Racing Car by Mercury, Italy; MRN 55, dating from 1960. Finished in silver, with the number "66", this is a fairly simple model. Scarce. Length: 4·016in (102mm).

23 Ferrari Supersqualo by Mercury, Italy; MRN 53, dating from 1960. Finished in red, this is another fairly basic model in 1:43 scale. Scarce. Length: 3·583in (91mm).

24 Mercedes Benz 196 Grand Prix Racing Car (Streamlined) by Mercury, Italy; MRN 56, dating from 1960. It is finished in silver, with the race number "48". Another scarce model. Length: 3·74in (95mm).

25 Lancia D.50 Grand Prix Racing Car by Mercury, Italy; MRN 54, dating from 1960. It is finished in red and bears the race number "92". Again, a scarce item from an early series. Length: 3·425in (87mm).

1 Ferrari Dino by Intercars, Spain;
dating from around 1970. Finished
in metallic blue, with a Ferrari
badge and the race number "27",
this model features opening doors
and basic moulded interior.
Length: 4·6875in (119mm).
2 Porsche GT Le Mans by Dalia
Solido; Spain; makers' reference
number (MRN) 134, dated (on
base) March 1964. Finished in silver,
with a black, red and gold trim strip
(West German national colours)
and the race number "30", this
model has opening doors and a
detailed interior (left-hand drive).
Length: 3·622in (92mm).
3 Ferrari 330 P2 by Mercury, Italy;
dating from around 1968-70.
Finished in yellow, with a red,
white and green strip (Italian
national colours) and the race

number "24", this is a very well-
detailed model, with plated wing-
mirrors and windscreen wiper;
opening doors and a moulded
interior (right-hand drive); and
a rear cover that lifts off, as
seen here, to show a fully-detailed
engine and a rear-mounted spare
wheel. Length: 3·819in (97mm).
4 Fiat Abarth 1000 by Dalia
Solido, Spain; MRN 124, dated (on
base) September 1962. Finished
in silver, with a red-and-white strip,
and the race number "5", this
model has opening doors and a
detailed interior (left-hand drive).
Length: 3·189in (81mm).
5 Aston Martin DB4 by Corgi Toys,
Great Britain; MRN 309, first
issued in 1962 and available until
1965. Appearing only in green-and-
white, with the race numbers "3"

or "1", this model features a
bonnet that opens to show a detailed
engine, a moulded interior (right-
hand drive), jewelled headlights,
and a suspension system. It is
one of the less common items in
Corgi's range of racing and rally
cars. Length: 3·74in (95mm).
6 Alfa Romeo Giulia T2 by Dalia
Solido, Spain; MRN 148, dated (on
base) June 1966. Finished in red
with white trim, with the race
number "82", this model features
headlights with coloured plastic
lenses, opening doors, and a
detailed interior (left-hand drive).
Length: 3·504in (89mm).
7 Fiat Abarth 1000 Bialbero by
Mercury, Italy; dating from 1966.
Finished in silver, with a badge
and the race number "182", this
model has opening doors, a

detailed moulded interior (left-hand
drive), and an opening boot.
Length: 4·3125in (110mm).
8 Ferrari Racing Sports Car by
Tekno, Denmark; MRN 813, dating
from 1958. In red-and-cream
finish that incorporates the Danish
emblem, with the race number
"5", this simple but attractive
model has an open cockpit with a
clear plastic windscreen and a
driver wearing racing overalls.
Length: 3·74in (95mm).
9 DB Panhard Le Mans by Dalia
Solido, Spain; dating from the
1960s. Finished in blue, with a
tricolour strip (French national
colours) and the race number "46",
this model has an open cockpit
with a wraparound plastic windscreen and a driver (right-hand
drive) in racing overalls and red

helmet. Length: 3·307in (84mm).
10 Ferrari 2·5-Litre by Dalia Solido, Spain; MRN 129, dated January 1964. Finished in red, with badges and the race number "152", this has a body casting incorporating front air vents and a rear spoiler; the detailed cockpit, with wraparound plastic windscreen, holds an overalled, helmeted driver (right-hand drive). Length: 3·622in (92mm).

11-12 Ferrari Racing Sports Car by Mercury, Italy; dating from around 1970. Two versions are shown. The car at (11) is finished in British racing green (note the Union flag on the rear compartment cover, shown here removed), with badges and the race number "18". The car at (12) is finished in metallic silver and red, with the race number "4". The model has a detailed open cockpit with driver (right-hand drive), opening doors, and a rear cover (with cast air intake) that is removable, showing a fully-detailed engine and a spare wheel. Length: 3·74in (95mm).

13 Lancia D24 by Mercury, Italy; MRN N26, dating from 1960. Finished in red with the race number "84", this is a plain and simple model with a fairly basically-detailed body casting. Length: 3·622in (92mm).

14 Aston Martin 3L DBRI 300 by Solido, France; dating from the 1960s. Finished in green with the race number "2", this model has details of vents and fairings incorporated into its body casting. It has an open cockpit with an overalled driver (right-hand drive) behind a wraparound windscreen. Length: 3·622in (92mm).

15 Aston Martin 3L by Dalia Solido, Spain; dating from the 1960s. It is interesting to compare this model, finished in yellow, with that of the same car issued by Solido, France; shown at (14). The same body casting is used for the model issued by the Spanish company: only the wheels are different. Length: 3·622in (92mm).

16 Jaguar Le Mans "D" Type by Solido, France; dating from the 1960s. Finished in dark green with the race number "8", this has a body casting that incorporates a tail-fin. The overalled, helmeted driver is protected by a clear plastic wraparound windscreen. Length: 3·622in (92mm).

17 Dino Sport by Mercury, Italy; dating from the 1960s. Finished in red with the race number "186", this is fitted with opening doors and boot; the cast cockpit, with the rather crude figure of a driver, also houses a moulded plastic engine. Length: 3·622in (92mm).

18 Porsche Spyder by Dalia Solido, Spain; dating from the 1960s. Finished in silver with the race number "5", this features a plastic canopy over the right side only of the left-hand-drive cockpit. Length: 3·386in (86mm).

19 Ferrari Type 500 TRC by Dalia Solido, Spain; dating from the 1960s. Finished in red, with badges and the race number "4", this has a detailed cockpit with driver (right-hand drive) and a clear plastic wraparound windscreen. Length: 3·74in (95mm).

1 Ferrari P312 by Mercury, Italy; dating from 1966. Finished in white, with applied badges and trim strips and the race number "9", this model features an opening rear engine compartment with a basically-detailed engine. It has a suspension system and wide speedwheels. Length: 3·898in (99mm).

2 Ferrari 330 P4 by Mercury, Italy; dating from 1966. Finished in red, with applied badges and the number "19", this model has opening doors, an opening rear engine compartment with a detailed engine, and a detailed cockpit with a clear plastic canopy that is fitted with a windscreen wiper. A suspension system is fitted. Length: 3·898in (99mm).

3 Ferrari 250 Le Mans Pininfarina by Politoys, Italy; maker's reference number (MRN) 525, dating from 1967. Finished in red, with a white-and-red strip and the number "12", this model features an opening bonnet, doors and boot, a detailed interior, and suspension. Length: 3·819in (97mm).

4 Ferrari Open Sports Car by Gama, West Germany; MRN 9610, dating from 1963. Finished in metallic green with the number "7", this fairly simple model, fitted with a suspension system, is from the maker's "Mini" range of vehicles. Length: 3·74in (95mm).

5 Maserati Sports Car by Dinky Toys, France; French Dinky Toys Reference Number 22a, dating from 1958. Finished in red, it has a well-modelled radiator complete with marque badge, cast headlights and filler caps, a clear plastic windscreen, and a driver (left-hand drive) in racing overalls. Its chromed metal wheels are fitted with detachable rubber tyres. Length: 3·425in (87mm).

6 Maserati 3500 GT by Mercury, Italy; MRN 24, dating from 1964. Finished in red, with applied strips and badges and the number "48", this model has an opening bonnet and boot and a detailed plastic interior (left-hand drive). A suspension system is fitted. Length: 4·252in (108mm).

7 Howmet "TX" Sports Racing Car by Politoys, Italy; MRN M10, dating from c1970. Finished in metallic green with a red strip and applied "TX" badges, this model is fitted with opening gull-wing doors and a rear compartment that opens to show a detailed engine. It is

fitted with plastic speedwheels. Length: 3·386in (86mm).

8 Porsche Carrera G by Mercury, Italy; dating from 1967. Finished in white, with a red bonnet and the number "18", this has an opening bonnet and opening gull-wing doors. Suspension is fitted. Length: 4·016in (102mm).

9-10 Porsche 917 by Mercury, Italy; dating from c1970. Two versions are shown: (9) is finished in metallic dark blue, with applied badges and the number "54"; (10) is in metallic pale blue with a red strip and bears the number "1". The model has dual headlights with clear plastic lenses. As shown at (10), the rear compartment opens upward to give access to the engine and rear-mounted spare wheel. Length: 4·016in (102mm).

11 Porsche 917 by Politoys, Italy;
MRN E18, dating from c1967.
Finished in metallic dark blue with
the number "3", this has a detailed
rear engine and is fitted with
suspension and speedwheels.
Length: 3·7in (94mm).
12 Porsche 908/03 by Mercury, Italy;
dating from c1966. Finished in
pale blue, with red trim and the
number "12", this has a rear
compartment that lifts to show a
well-detailed engine and spare
wheel. Length: 3·425in (87mm).
13 Porsche 904 Carrera GTS by
Politoys, Italy; MRN 535, dating
from 1967. Finished in white, with a
yellow-and-black strip and the
number "9", this features a bonnet
that opens to show a plated plastic
tool kit, opening doors and a
detailed interior (left-hand drive),

and an opening rear engine
compartment. Suspension is fitted
at the rear. Length: 3·74in (95mm).
14 Alfa Romeo 33 by Mercury, Italy;
dating from c1966. Finished in
red, with applied badges and the
number "9", it has an opening
bonnet (note that the casting
incorporates air vents), opening
doors, a detailed open cockpit
(left-hand drive) with a roll-over bar,
and a rear compartment that
opens to show a detailed engine.
Length: 3·74in (95mm).
15 Ford GT40 (or possibly a Lotus 30)
by Gama, West Germany; MRN
9603, dating from c1963. Finished
in metallic dark blue, with a
yellow bonnet, applied badges and
the number "7", it has an opening
bonnet, a detailed open cockpit
(right-hand drive) with a clear

plastic wraparound windscreen
and a plated roll-over bar behind,
and a detailed rear engine.
Length: 4·016in (102mm).
16 Ford Mark II by Mebetoys Mattel,
Italy; MRN 6607, dating from
c1968. Finished in metallic grey
with the number "2", it has an
opening bonnet and doors, a rear
compartment that opens to show a
detailed engine, and speedwheels.
Length: 3·74in (95mm).
17 Ford Mustang Boss 302 by
Mebetoys Mattel, Italy; MRN 6611,
dating from c1968. Finished in
silver, with applied badges and the
number "6", it has a bonnet
that opens to show a detailed
engine, opening doors and a
detailed interior, a louvred rear
window, and an opening boot with
a spoiler. It is fitted with speedwheels.

Length: 4·37in (111mm).
18 Ford GTJ by Politoys, Italy; MRN
586, dating from 1968. Finished
in white with the number "2", it has
opening doors and is fitted with
speedwheels and suspension.
Length: 3·898in (99mm).
19 Ford Lola GT by Politoys, Italy; MRN
534, dating from 1967. Finished
in metallic dark blue, with a white-
and-red strip and the number
"4", it has opening doors and a
detailed interior (right-hand drive),
a rear engine beneath a clear plastic
cover, and front-wheel suspension.
Length: 3·5625in (90mm).
20 Lola Aston Martin by Politoys,
Italy; MRN 565, dating from 1968.
Finished in pale green, with a
chequered strip and the number
"4", it is fitted with speedwheels.
Length: 3·898in (99mm).

1 **Ferrari 312T Grand Prix Racing Car** by Super Champion, France; dating from the 1960s-70s. Finished in red and white, with applied badges and the race number "12", this model, like the other cars in the maker's "Champion" series shown at (2), (3) and (4), is made to a scale of 1:66. Like all the "Champion" Grand Prix cars, it has a metal body and a plastic chassis and is fitted with fat plastic "rocket wheels". Length: 4·016in (102mm).

2 **Ligier J.S.5 Grand Prix Racing Car** by Super Champion, France; dating from the 1960-70s. Finished in blue, white and cream, with applied badges and the race number "26", this model is of the same construction as (1). Details include black plastic wing mirrors and a realistic representation of the rear

suspension and exhaust system. Length: 3·819in (97mm).

3-4 **Tyrell P34-2 Grand Prix Racing Car** by Super Champion, France; dating from the 1960s-70s. Both examples shown are finished in dark blue with yellow trim, with applied badges. The car shown at (3) bears the race number "3", and has an exposed rear engine, detailed in black plastic, and a cast front spoiler. The car shown at (4) bears the race number "4": it has a cast cover fitted over its engine compartment and additional plastic detail on its front spoiler. Both versions feature six plastic "rocket wheels". Length: 3·819in (97mm).

5 **Porsche 917L Le Mans Sports Racing Car, "Ecurie Gulf John Wyer"**, by Super Champion, France; maker's reference number (MRN)

64, dating from the 1960s-70s. Finished in pale blue, with a black-and-orange trim strip, applied badges and the race number "18", this model, like all the cars shown at (6-15), is from the maker's "Super Champions" series and is made to a scale of 1:43. All these cars have well-detailed plastic bodies in authentic racing team colour finishes, with many transfers that reproduce the sponsors' badges that are a feature of all cars on the international racing circuits today. All the cars in this series have metal bases, and all have wheels fitted with treaded plastic tyres. On this model and the other "Super Champions" shown here, note also the clear plastic-lensed headlights and the clear plastic windows, with a windscreen incorporating details

of wipers and—in the models shown at (5-9)—rear-view mirrors. The photograph at *Inset (above right)* shows how these models were marketed—in clear plastic display boxes with card bases that featured a description of their prototypes' international racing triumphs. Length: 4·488in (114mm).

6 **Porsche 917H Le Mans Sports Racing Car, "Martini Racing Team"**, by Super Champion, France; MRN 65, dating from the 1960s-70s. Finished in dark blue, pale blue, silver and red, with the race number "21". All other details of construction are as described at (5). Length: 4·488in (114mm).

7 **Porsche 917L Le Mans Sports Racing Car, "International Martini Racing Team"**, by Super Champion, France; MRN 50, dating from the

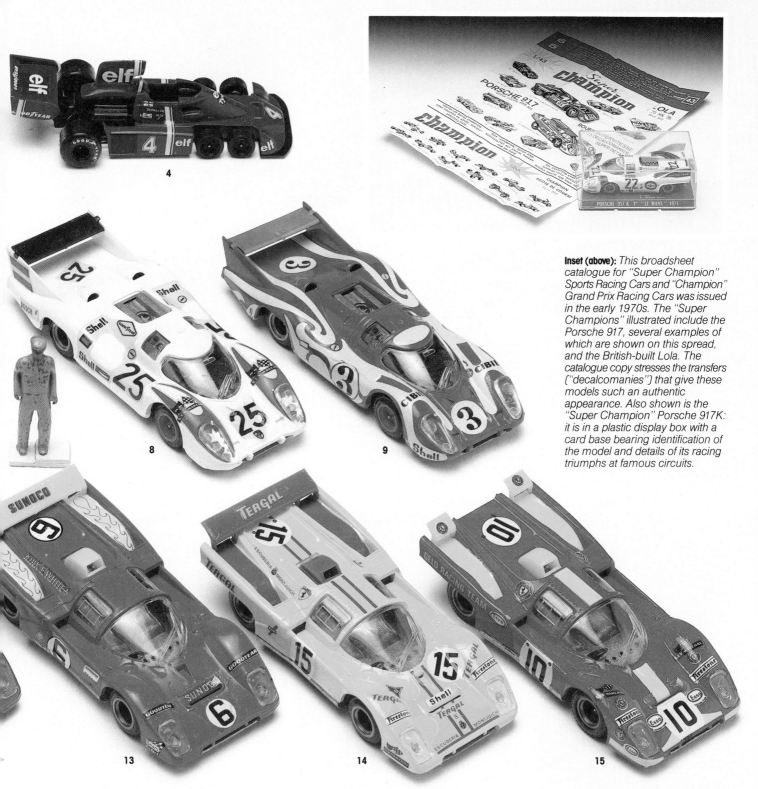

Inset (above): *This broadsheet catalogue for "Super Champion" Sports Racing Cars and "Champion" Grand Prix Racing Cars was issued in the early 1970s. The "Super Champions" illustrated include the Porsche 917, several examples of which are shown on this spread, and the British-built Lola. The catalogue copy stresses the transfers ("decalcomanies") that give these models such an authentic appearance. Also shown is the "Super Champion" Porsche 917K: it is in a plastic display box with a card base bearing identification of the model and details of its racing triumphs at famous circuits.*

1960s-70s. Finished in dark blue, green and cream, this model bears the race number "3". All other details of construction are as described at (5). Length: 4·488in (114mm).

8 Porsche 917L Le Mans Sports Racing Car, "Le Mans 70", by Super Champion, France; MRN 52, dating from the 1970s. Finished in white, with red trim and the usual applied badges, this model bears the race number "25". All other details of construction are as described at (5). Length: 4·488in (114mm).

9 Porsche 917L Le Mans Sports Racing Car, "Essais Lemans", by Super Champion, France; MRN 51, dating from the 1960s-70s. Finished in dark blue and cream, this model bears the race number "3". All other details of construction are as described at (5). Length: 4·488in (114mm).

10 Ferrari 512M Sports Racing Car, "Filipinetti" by Super Champion, France; MRN 65, dating from the 1960s-70s. Finished in red, with cream and blue trim, this model bears the race number "6". Like the versions of the Porsche 917L and 917H shown at (5-9), it has a plastic body, metal chassis, and wheels with treaded plastic tyres. It has headlights with lenses of clear plastic and clear plastic windows, with a windscreen incorporating detail of wipers. Note that the design of the plastic rear spoilers varies from car to car in the examples shown at (10-15). Length: 3·898in (99mm).

11 Ferrari 512M Sports Racing Car, "Francorchamps", by Super Champion, France; MRN 60, dating from the 1960s-70s. Finished in yellow with red trim, this model bears the race number "9". All other details of construction are as (10). Length: 3·898in (99mm).

12 Ferrari 512M Sports Racing Car, "N.A.R.T." (North American Racing Team), by Super Champion, France; MRN 64, dating from the 1960s-70s. Finished in red with cream-and-black trim, this model bears the race number "12". All other details of construction are as described at (10). Length: 3·898in (99mm).

13 Ferrari 512M Sports Racing Car, "Sunoco" by Super Champion, France; MRN 61, dating from the 1960s-70s. Finished in dark blue with yellow and red trim, this model bears the race number "6". All other details of construction are as (10). Length: 3·898in (99mm).

14 Ferrari 512M Sports Racing Car, "Montjuich", by Super Champion,

France; MRN 62, dating from the 1960s-70s. Finished in yellow with green and red trim, this model bears the race number "15". All other details of construction are as (10). Length: 3·898in (99mm).

15 Ferrari 512M Sports Racing Car, "Gelo Racing Team", by Super Champion, France; MRN 63, dating from the 1960s-70s. Finished in red with yellow trim, this model bears the race number "10". All other details of construction are as (10). Like all the Super Champion cars shown on this spread, this model may now prove quite hard to find, since the range appeared only for a relatively brief period in the late 1960s and early 1970s. Further information on the series is given in the introductory note on *pages 100-101.* Length: 3·898in (99mm).

Super Champion models were aimed specifically at motor racing enthusiasts, and fall into the category of toys for adults rather than children. They were made in France for a relatively short period, in the late 1960s and early 1970s, and although not particularly expensive at the time of issue, they are now popular collector's items and may prove hard to find.

The models are made to a scale of 1:43. Smaller models of Grand Prix cars, made to a scale of 1:66, were produced in the same maker's "Champion" series; examples are shown at (1-4) on *pages 98-99*. These models of sports racing cars have well-detailed plastic bodies, finished in the near-authentic liveries of famous racing teams (or even in the colours worn in specific races

at wellknown circuits), with a wealth of sponsors' advertising, and metal chassis. (The "Champion" models of Grand Prix cars, it should be noted, have metal bodies and are fitted with plastic chassis.)

1 Porsche 917 Sports Racing Car, "Martini Racing Team" (Kayalami), by Super Champion, France; maker's reference number (MRN) 55, dating from the 1960s-70s. Finished in yellow, with red and cream trim and the race number "2", this model carries the usual wealth of transfers. In common with the other cars shown on this spread, it has a well-detailed plastic body finished in authentic racing team livery, a metal chassis and treaded plastic tyres. Note the headlights with clear plastic lenses, the clear

plastic windows (on this example; some have tinted plastic windows) with a windscreen incorporating details of a wiper and rear-view mirror, and the detail on the upper rear body of an engine with cooling fan. Length: 4·488in (114mm).
2 Porsche 917 Sports Racing Car, "Temporada", by Super Champion, France; MRN 40, dating from the 1960s-70s. Finished in white, with cream and green trim, this model bears the race number "28". All other details are as (1).
3 Porsche 917 Sports Racing Car, "Le Mans", by Super Champion, France; MRN 43, dating from the 1960s-70s. Finished in orange, with cream trim, this model bears the race number "23". All other details are as described at (1).
4 Porsche 917 Sports Racing Car,

"Ecurie Hollandaise", by Super Champion, France; MRN 45, dating from the 1960s-70s. It is finished in yellow and bears the race number "18". All other details are as (1).
5 Porsche 917 Sports Racing Car, "Brands Hatch", by Super Champion, France; MRN 44, dating from the 1960s-70s. It is finished in blue, with dark green spoilers and cream trim, and bears the race number "12". All other details are as described at (1).
6 Porsche 917 Sports Racing Car, "Daytona", by Super Champion, France; MRN 41, dating from the 1960s-70s. This model is finished in white, with cream and red trim, and bears the race number "3". All other details of construction are as (1).
7 Porsche 917K Sports Racing Car, "Martini & Rossi Racing Team" (12-

hour Sebring), by Super Champion, France; MRN 62, dating from the 1960s-70s. Finished in silver, with red and blue trim, this bears the race number "3". All other details of construction are as (1).

8 Porsche 917 Sports Racing Car, "Monza", by Super Champion, France; MRN 42, dating from the 1960s-70s. Finished in blue, with black and orange trim, this bears the number "7". All other details of construction are as (1).

9 Porsche 917 Sports Racing Car, "David Piper", by Super Champion, France; MRN 54, dating from the 1960s-70s. Finished in orange, with silver trim, this bears the number "3". All others details are as (1).

10 Porsche 917 Sports Racing Car, "Hockenheim 70", by Super Champion, France; MRN 53, dating

from the 1960s-70s. Finished in blue, with green and cream trim, this bears the race number "12". All other details are as (1).

11 Lola T70 Mk 3B Sports Racing Car, "Grand Prix d'Autriche", by Super Champion, France; MRN 31, dating from the 1960s-70s. Finished in green, this model of a British-built car bears the race number "32". All details of construction are as (1). Length: 4·8125in (122mm).

12 Lola T70 Mk 3B Sports Racing Car, "Nurburgring", by Super Champion, France; MRN 34, dating from the 1960s-70s. Finished in yellow, with red and white trim, this bears the race number "55". All other details of construction are as (1).

13 Lola T70 Mk 3B Sports Racing Car, "Temporada" (Buenos Aires), by Super Champion, France; MRN 30,

dating from the 1960s-70s. Finished in red, with blue and white trim, this bears the race number "50". All other details as (1).

14 Porsche 917K Sports Racing Car, "Ecurie Gulf John Wyer", by Super Champion, France; MRN 61, dating from the 1960s-70s. It is finished in blue, with black and orange trim, and bears the race number "19". All other details as (1) — but note the added tail fins on this model and those at (15) and (16).

15 Porsche 917K Sports Racing Car, "Le Mans 1971", by Super Champion, France; MRN 60, dating from the 1960s-70s. Finished in white, with blue and red trim, this bears the race number "22". All other details of construction are as (1).

16 Porsche 917K Sports Racing Car, "Nurburgring", by Super Champion,

France; MRN 63, dating from the 1960s-70s. Finished in yellow with green trim, this bears the number "55". All other details as (1).

17 Lola T70 Mk 3B Sports Racing Car, "Monza", by Super Champion, France; MRN 35, dating from the 1960s-70s. Finished in white, with green trim, this bears the race number "33". All other details as (1).

18 Lola T70 Mk 3B Sports Racing Car, "1,000-Km de Paris", by Super Champion, France; MRN 32, dating from the 1960s-70s. Finished in blue, with pale green, yellow and white trim, this bears the race number "102". All other details as (1).

19 Lola T70 Mk 3B Sports Racing Car, "24 Hours Daytona", by Super Champion, France; MRN 33, dating from the 1960s-70s. All details of construction are as (1).

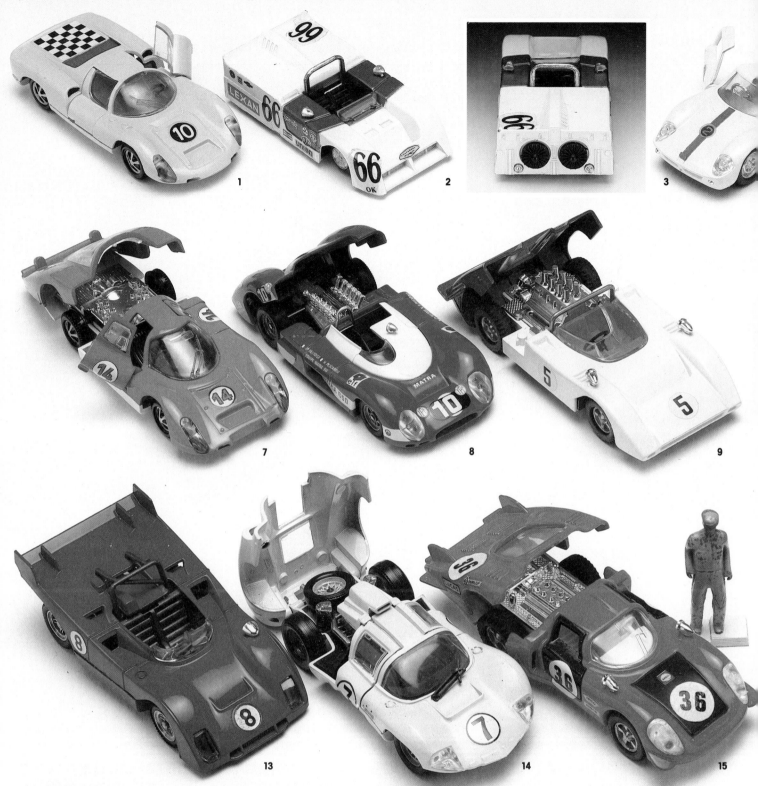

1Porsche 910 by Märklin, West Germany; dating from the 1960s-70s. Finished in pale green, with chequered trim and the race number "100", this model features opening doors, plastic-lensed headlights and clear plastic windows, and a detailed interior (left-hand drive). Length: 3·622in (92mm).
2Chaparral Can-Am 2J by Mercury, Italy; dating from the 1960s-70s. Finished in white, with applied badges and the number "66", this model is fitted with bright-plated rear-view mirrors and roll-over bar; and, as seen in the close-up rear view at *Inset,* plastic details of turbo-fans at the rear of the car. Length: 3·268in (83mm).
3Ford Lola GT by Politoys, Italy; maker's reference number (MRN) 534, dating from the 1960s-70s.

Finished in white, with a red strip and the number "2", this model has opening doors, a detailed interior, and clear plastic headlight lenses, windows and a rear compartment cover. Length: 3·504in (89mm).
4Ferrari 312P by Dinky Toys, Great Britain; Dinky Toys Reference Number (DT No) 204, first issued in 1971 and available until 1974. Appearing only in red body finish, and also with the race number "60", this model has upward-opening doors and is fitted with speedwheels. It is fairly easily available. Length: 3·898in (99mm).
5Ford Le Mans by Solido, France; MRN 146, dated (on base) March 1966. Finished in white, with dark blue bonnet and trim strips and the number "12", this has a basically-detailed interior and an opening

boot. Length: 3·74in (95mm).
6Lola T212 by Mebetoys Mattel, Italy; dating from around 1970. Finished in metallic green, with chequered trim, applied badges and the number "8", this has a body that lifts up (pivoting at the front end) to show details of cockpit and engine. Length: 3·622in (92mm).
7Porsche 907 by Märklin, West Germany; dating from the 1960s-70s. Finished in orange with the number "14", this well-detailed model has headlights with clear plastic lenses, opening doors, a detailed interior, and a rear compartment that lifts to show details of a well-modelled engine. Length: 4·252in (108mm).
8Matra 650 by Solido, France; MRN 176, dated (on base) June 1970. Finished in blue, with applied badges

and the number "10", this is fitted with a plated rear-view mirror and has a rear compartment cover that lifts to show a fully-detailed engine. Length: 3·819in (97mm).
9McLaren M8A Can-Am by Dinky Toys, Great Britain; DT No 233, first issued in 1971 and available until 1974. Finished in white-and-blue (and appearing also in other colour schemes), with the race number "5", this model has plated rear-view mirrors and a rear compartment that lifts to show a detailed engine. It is a fairly common model. Length: 3·7in (94mm).
10McLaren M8D by Mebetoys Mattel, Italy; MRN 6626, dating from the 1960s-70s. Finished in orange, with a black spoiler, applied badges and the number "4", this model has an upward-lifting front and rear that

open on to a very well-detailed engine, cockpit and chassis. Length: 3·74in (95mm).

11 Porsche 908/03 by Mercury, Italy; dating from the 1960s-70s. Finished in white, with applied badges and the number "22", this has a detailed cockpit, with roll-over bar, and a rear compartment that lifts up to show a well-detailed engine and a spare wheel. Length: 3·504in (89mm).

12 Ferrari P312 by Mercury, Italy; dating from the 1960s-70s. Finished in red, with applied badges and the number "8", this model has a rear compartment that lifts to show a well-detailed bright-plated engine and a realistic exhaust system. Length: 3·819in (97mm).

13 Ferrari 313PB by Mebetoys Mattel, Italy; MRN 8553, dating from the 1960s-70s. Finished in red with the

number "8", this has a simple but effective body casting, incorporating vents and rear fins, and is fitted with a plated rear view mirror, headlight lenses and windscreen of tinted plastic, and a detailed plastic cockpit with roll-over bars behind. Length: 3·622in (92mm).

14 Chaparral 2D by Solido, France; MRN 153, dated (on base) November 1967. Finished in white with the race number "7", this is a most attractive model, with opening gull-wing doors and rear engine compartment (showing engine and spare wheel), and a cast roof-mounted air intake. Length: 3·74in (95mm).

15 Alfa Romeo 33 by Dinky Toys, Great Britain; DT No 210, first issued in 1971 and available until 1973. Seen here in red-and-black finish,

and appearing also in blue, with the race number "36", this model has plated mirrors, opening doors and a rear compartment that opens to show a well-detailed engine. It is fitted with speedwheels. It may be slightly harder to find than the similar models at (4) and (9). Length: 4·21in (107mm).

16 Porsche Carrera 6 by Solido, France; MRN 151, dated (on base) May 1967. Finished in silver-blue, with a red bonnet and the race number "37", this simple but effective model has plated mirrors, opening doors, and clear plastic headlight lenses, windows and rear engine compartment cover. Length: 3·7in (94mm).

17 Chaparral 2F by Solido, France; MRN 169, dated (on base) May 1968. Finished in white, with the race

number "7", this model has an attractive and well-detailed body casting, incorporating opening gull-wing doors and a rear-mounted cast metal aerofoil. It is fitted with clear plastic headlight lenses and a clear plastic windscreen. Length: 3·504in (89mm).

18 Alpine Renault 3L by Solido, France; MRN 168, dated (on base) April 1969. Finished in blue; with a tricolour trim strip, applied badges and the race number "30", this model has a simple but attractive body casting that incorporates opening doors and boot. It is fitted with clear plastic headlight lenses and windows (the windscreen with details of a wiper and rear-view mirror) and a clear plastic cover over the rear engine compartment. Length: 3·898in (99mm).

1 Ford Mirage by Politoys, Italy; maker's reference number (MRN) E15, dating from the 1960s-70s. Finished in metallic blue, with black-and-white chequered trim strips and the number "2", this is a fairly simple model with an open, detailed cockpit, complete with a clear plastic wraparound windscreen and a bright-plated rear engine. Like a number of the other models by Politoys shown on this spread, it is fitted with plastic speedwheels. Length: 3·898in (99mm).

2 Alfa Romeo 33 by Politoys, Italy; MRN 583, dating from the 1960s-70s. Finished in red, with applied badges and the number "182", this model has a detailed cockpit with clear plastic windows (the windscreen incorporating detail of wiper), and an opening rear engine compartment with detailed engine. Length: 3·622in (92mm).

3 B.R.M. P154 Can-Am by Politoys, Italy; MRN E34, dating from the 1960s-70s. Finished in white, with applied badges and the number "2", this model has a basically-detailed engine and a rear-mounted plastic spoiler. Length: 4·016in (102mm).

4 Abarth 3000 by Politoys, Italy; MRN 594, dating from the 1960s-70s. Finished in red, with applied badges and trim strips and the number "8", this model features a detailed cockpit and detailed rear engine. Length: 3·622in (92mm).

5 Porsche Audi 917-10 Can-Am by Politoys, Italy; MRN E39, dating from the 1960s-70s. Finished in white and red, with applied badges and the number "6", this has a basically-detailed cockpit with

roll-over bar and a body casting that incorporates details of fairings and a cast metal rear spoiler. Length: 3·898in (99mm).

6 McLaren Chevrolet M8F Can-Am by Politoys, Italy; MRN E32, dating from the 1960s-70s. Finished in yellow, with applied badges but no number, this features a cockpit with roll-over bar, a detailed rear engine and a black plastic rear spoiler. Length: 4·016in (102mm).

7 Matra Sport 630 by Politoys, Italy; MRN 595, dating from the 1960s-70s. Finished in blue, with applied badges and the number "2", this has an opening bonnet (with spare wheel), doors and rear engine compartment (with detailed engine); a detailed cockpit; and headlights fitted with clear plastic lenses. Length: 4·055in (103mm).

8 Alpine Renault by Politoys, Italy; MRN 598, dating from the 1960s-70s. Finished in blue, with applied badges and the number "28", this has an opening bonnet, doors and rear engine compartment (with clear plastic cover); a detailed cockpit; and headlights with clear plastic lenses. Length: 4·134in (105mm).

9 Ferrari Dino Berlinetta by Politoys, Italy; MRN 569, dating from the 1960s-70s. Finished in red, with neither badges nor number, this has upward-opening doors of clear plastic, a detailed cockpit, and plastic front and rear spoilers. The body casting incorporates considerable detail of air intakes and vents. Length: 3·819in (97mm).

10 Chevron GTB 16 by Politoys, Italy; MRN M21, dating from the 1960s-

70s. Finished in silver, with applied badges and the number "2", this has opening doors and a rear engine compartment with a detailed engine. Length: 3·898in (99mm).

11 Porsche 917 Le Mans by Politoys, Italy; MRN M20, dating from the 1960s-70s. Finished in red with the race number "2", this has upward-opening doors and a rear engine compartment that opens to show a detailed engine. The headlights have tinted plastic lenses; the windscreen (with wiper detail) and the engine compartment cover are likewise made of tinted plastic. Length: 4·252in (108mm).

12 Matra Simca Sports 660 by Politoys, Italy; MRN M16, dating from the 1960s-70s. Finished in blue, with applied badges and the number "8", this has upward-opening doors

and rear engine compartment (with plated roll-over bar) and a detailed engine. Length: 3·898in (99mm).

13 Lola 260 Can-Am by Politoys, Italy; MRN E33, dating from the 1960s-70s. Finished in white, with applied badges and the number "2", this is fitted with a black plastic roll-over bar and rear spoiler and a detailed rear-mounted engine. Length: 3·819in (97mm).

14 Serenissima by Politoys, Italy; MRN M15, dating from the 1960s-70s. Finished in silver, with the number "84", this features opening doors and a rear engine compartment (with detailed engine); tinted plastic headlight lenses and windscreen (with wiper detail). Length: 3·898in (99mm).

15 March 717-1 Can-Am by Politoys, Italy; MRN M26, dating from the

1960s-70s. Finished in red with the number "3", this has opening doors and rear engine compartment (with plated roll-over cage) and bright-plated rear-view mirrors. Length: 3·74in (95mm).

16 Ferrari 512S by Politoys, Italy; dating from the 1960s-70s. Finished in red and cream, with applied badges and the number "11", this has upward-opening doors and tinted plastic windows fitted. Length: 3·7in (94mm).

17 Lola T222 Can-Am by Politoys, Italy; MRN E35, dating from the 1960s-70s. Finished in gold, with applied trim strips and the number "4", this is fitted with a roll-over bar and a detailed rear engine. Length: 3·622in (92mm).

18 Alfa Romeo 33-3 by Mebetoys Mattel, Italy; MRN 6612, dating from

the 1970s. Finished in red, with badges and the number "2", this model has an opening bonnet, doors and boot and is fitted with bright-plated rear-view mirrors and filler caps. Length: 3·622in (92mm).

19 Abarth 3000SP by Mebetoys Mattel, Italy; MRN 6624, dating from the 1970s. Finished in red, with applied badges and the number "1", this has upward-opening doors and a rear engine compartment with a detailed engine beneath it. Length: 2·992in (76mm).

20 Ferrari Can-Am by Mebetoys Mattel, Italy; dating from c1970. Finished in red, with applied badges and the number "8", this has upward-opening doors, a spoiler behind the cockpit, and a rear compartment that opens to show a detailed engine. Length: 3·7in (94mm).

1 Porsche 917 by Solido, France; maker's reference number (MRN) 186, dated (on base) March 1971. Finished in red with cream trim, with applied badges and the race number "23", this model is fitted with clear plastic headlight lenses and windows (the windscreen incorporating wiper detail). It has a plastic diecast chassis with a suspension system. Length: 3·898in (99mm).

2 Ford Mark IV by Solido, France; MRN 170, dated (on base) February 1969. Finished in metallic red with white trim, with the race number "1", this model features plated rear-view mirrors and a black plastic windscreen wiper. It has clear plastic windows and rear compartment cover, and a detailed interior. The chassis is of anodised metal and a suspension system is fitted.

Length: 4·016in (102mm).
3 Lola T280 by Solido, France; MRN 15, dated (on base) April 1973. Finished in yellow, with applied badges and the race number "7", this model has clear plastic-lensed head- and spot-lights, a plated rear-view mirror, a plated roll-over bar behind the open cockpit, and basic detail of a rear engine. It has a plastic chassis with suspension. Length: 3·74in (95mm).
4 Ferrari 312 PB by Solido, France; MRN 194, dated (on base) May 1972. Finished in red, with applied badges and the race number "51", the model is fitted with a plated mirror and has a black roll-over bar behind its open cockpit. It has an anodised metal chassis with suspension. Length: 3·386in (86mm).
5 Porsche 917 by Solido, France;

MRN 198/186, dating from the early 1970s. Finished in white, with black-blue-and-red trim, applied badges and the race number "22", this model has a body casting that incorporates tail-fins. It has a plastic chassis with a suspension system. Length: 3·898in (99mm).
6 March 707 Can-Am by Solido, France; MRN 199, dated (on base) July 1972. Finished in red, with applied badges and the race number "77", this model has bright-plated rear-view mirrors, roll-over bar and basic rear engine detail. It has a plastic chassis with a suspension system. Length: 4·016in (102mm).
7 Ferrari 330 P3 by Solido, France; MRN 152, dated (on base) June 1967. Finished in red, with the race number "14", this model features an opening rear compartment with a

spare wheel and basic detail of engine and exhaust. It has an anodised metal chassis with suspension. Length: 3·74in (95mm).
8 Ligier JS/3 by Solido, France; MRN 195, dated (on base) March 1972. Finished in yellow with green trim, with applied badges and the race number "24", this model has a grey plastic cockpit surround, a bright-plated roll-over bar, and a rear compartment that lifts to show basic engine detail. It has an anodised metal chassis which is fitted with a suspension system. Length: 3·504in (89mm).
9 McLaren M8B Can-Am by Solido, France; MRN 176 dated (on base) March 1970. Finished in orange, with applied badges and the race number "4", this model has a bright-plated roll-over bar and basic

rear engine detail, and a rear airfoil in white plastic. It has a plastic chassis with a suspension system. Length: 3·74in (95mm).

10 Porsche 917 by Mercury, Italy; dating from the 1960s-70s. It is interesting to compare this model, finished in yellow with red trim and bearing the race number "12", with the very similar model by Solido, shown at (1). The Mercury version is a little larger and has a more detailed bright-plated rear engine under a lift-up compartment cover. Length: 4·016in (102mm).

11 Alfa Romeo 33/3 by Solido, France; MRN 187, dated (on base) April 1971. Finished in red, with the race number "37", this has a very well-detailed body casting, with a lift-up rear compartment cover complete with spoiler. It has a plastic

chassis with a suspension system. Length: 4·016in (102mm).

12 Porsche Carrera G by Mercury, Italy; dating from the 1960s-70s. Finished in white, with an orange bonnet and the race number "18", this has clear plastic headlight lenses, windows and lifting rear engine compartment cover. Length: 4·016in (102mm).

13 Porsche 917/10 TC Can-Am by Solido, France; MRN 18, dated (on base) July 1973. Finished in white, with red-and-black trim, applied badges and the race number "7", it has a well-detailed body casting, with a rear airfoil, and is fitted with a detachable rear engine cover. Note the plated rear-view mirrors and roof-mounted fan in yellow plastic. Length: 4·016in (102mm).

14 Lola T70 Mark 3B by Solido, France;

MRN 175, dated (on base) January 1970. Finished in red with applied badges and the race number "6", this model has opening doors and basic rear engine detail. It has an anodised metal chassis to which a suspension sytem is fitted. Length: 3·74in (95mm).

15 Ferrari 512S by Solido, France; MRN 182, dated (on base) September 1970. Finished in yellow, with a white rear cover and the race number "28", it has clear plastic windows, opening doors and an anodised metal chassis with suspension. Length: 3·7in (94mm).

16 Ferrari 512M by Solido, France; MRN 197, dated (on base) July 1972. Finished in metallic blue, with yellow rear trim, a silver airfoil and a white air intake, with applied badges and the race number "11", this is fitted with

opening doors. Note the plated rear-view mirror applied to the clear plastic windscreen. It has an anodised metal chassis with suspension. Length: 4·016in (102mm).

17 Ferrari 312P by Solido, France; MRN 177, dated (on base) April 1970. Finished in red, with applied badges and the race number "18", this model has a plastic chassis with a suspension system fitted. Length: 3·898in (99mm).

18 Porsche 908 by Solido, France; MRN 174, dated (on base) November 1969. Finished in white, with red trim, applied badges and the race number "64", this model features opening doors and a rear spoiler. It has clear plastic windows and rear compartment cover, and a plastic chassis with suspension. Length: 4·37in (111mm).

1 B.M.W. 2002 Turbo by Solido, France; maker's reference number (MRN) 28, dated October 1975. (Note that all the cars in this series have a date—in the example shown, "10-75"—stamped on the base.) Like all the models on this spread, it represents a left-hand drive car and is made to a scale of 1:43. Finished in metallic grey, with red-and-blue "Turbo" side trim strip, this model has a number plate, "M-KM 1843", applied front and rear. It has bright metal headlights, red plastic rearlights and sculptured plastic wheels and tyres. The metal base has cast details of transmission, exhaust and suspension. Length: 3·858in (98mm).

2 B.M.W. 530; MRN 89, dated July 1979. Finished in metallic grey, with applied make and rally badges

and blue-and-red trim strips, this model has plastic windows (the driver's part-open); a detailed plastic interior, including a roll-cage at the rear; sculptured plastic wheels, and a plastic base with basic transmission details moulded in. Length: 4·055in (103mm).

3 Alfa Romeo Alfetta GTV; MRN 82, dated March 1979. Finished in white with a black bonnet, with applied badges and the number "31", this model features plastic windows and steering wheel; it has jewelled dual headlights and red-painted cast rearlights. Fitted with sculptured plastic wheels, it has a plastic base with transmission details. Length: 3·7in (94mm).

4 Opel Kadett Coupé GTE; MRN 70, dated November 1978. Finished in orange, with applied badges and

the number "31", this model has plastic windows and a detailed interior. Its front and rear bumpers and lights are of plated plastic. It has sculptured plastic wheels and a plastic base with basic details of suspension and exhaust moulded in. Length: 3·858in (98mm).

5 Toyota Celica; MRN 1094, dated March 1980. Finished in cream, with applied badges and the number "29", this car has an applied number plate, "E.1388", front and rear. It has plastic windows and a detailed interior with a roll-cage at the rear. The radiator and front and rear bumpers are inset plastic; the headlights and spots are bright metal. It has sculptured plastic wheels and tyres and a metal base with details of transmission and exhaust. Length: 3·858in (98mm).

6 Lancia Stratos; MRN 73, dated January 1979. Finished in white, with applied badges and the number "19", this features a plastic spoiler and louvred rear window. Note also the array of cast headlights. It has plastic wheels and a plain metal base. Length: 3·386in (86mm).

7 B.M.W. M1; MRN 1031, dated April 1981. Finished in dark blue, with applied badges and the number "41", this model has a diecast spoiler and a louvred plastic rear window. It has non-opening doors and inset plastic head- and rearlights. The wheels and the base, with basic suspension details, are plastic. Length: 4·17in (106mm).

8 Ford Capri 2600 RV; MRN 26, dated September 1974. Finished in metallic blue with white stripes, with applied badges and the number

"55", this features jewelled dual headlights and plastic rally lamps with covers on the front bumper. With opening doors, it is equipped with sculptured plastic wheels and is fitted with a plain plastic base. Length: 3·858in (98mm).

9 Peugeot 504 Coupé V6; MRN 1055, dated February 1980. Finished in white, with applied badges and the number "02", it has spotlights, front splash-guards and rear bumper of bright metal; the inset radiator, headlights and mud flaps on rear wheels are plastic. Its detailed plastic interior includes a rear roll-cage. It has sculptured plastic wheels and a plastic base with moulded details of transmission. Length: 3·937in (100mm).

10 B.M.W. 3.0 CLS; MRN 25, dated May 1974. Finished in white with

blue-and-red trim, the number "31" and applied badges, this model has bright metal headlights, red plastic rearlights and an inset plastic radiator. It has opening doors and a detailed interior with tip-up front seats. Its sculptured plastic wheels are fitted with fat, smooth plastic tyres. Its metal base is fully detailed. Length: 4·17mm (106mm).

11 Fiat Abarth 131 Rallye; MRN 54, dated November 1977. Finished in blue and yellow, with applied badges and the number "5", this model features a plastic rear spoiler, red plastic rearlights, and bright metal headlights and spots. Plastic windows are fitted all round and it has a detailed interior with a rear roll-cage. It has sculptured plastic wheels and a yellow metal base with cast detail of transmission and

black metal axle boxes and exhaust system. Length: 3·937in (100mm).

12 B.M.W. 3.0 CSL; MRN 75, dated June 1978. Finished in orange, with applied badges and the number "21", it has jewelled dual headlights and inset red plastic rearlights. It has opening doors and a detailed interior. With sculptured plastic wheels, it has a plastic base with details of transmission and exhaust. Length: 4·016in (102mm).

13 Ford Escort L; MRN 45, dated June 1976. Finished in white and black, with applied badges and the number "15", this has bright metal headlights and plated plastic spotlights and front and rear bumpers. It has a detailed interior, sculptured plastic wheels and is fitted with a plain plastic base. Length: 3·7in (94mm).

14 Renault 5 Turbo; MRN 1023, dated July 1981. Finished in metallic blue, with applied badges and the number "18", and applied number plates, "6891 VK 38", front and rear, this model has a blue plastic base that sweeps upward to incorporate details of sills and front and rear bumpers. Its detailed interior includes a plastic roll-cage. Length: 3·386in (86mm).

Inset (top right): *The bases of three of the Solido rally cars. (Left to right): the basically-detailed black plastic base of the Opel Kadett Coupé GTE (4); the yellow metal base of the Fiat Abarth 131 Rallye (11), bearing cast metal details of transmission, axle boxes and exhaust; and the plain black plastic base of the Ford Escort L (13).*

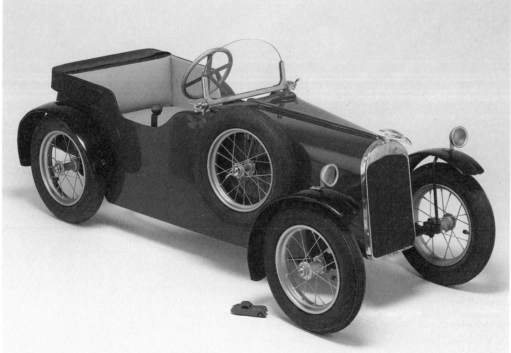

Left: "*Magna No 8*" *Pedal Car by Tri-ang (Lines Brothers Ltd), Great Britain; dating from the mid-1930s, when it was priced at £5 15s 0d (£5.75, $6.90). This representation of a British-built touring car, with a metal frame and wooden panels, was glowingly described in the maker's catalogue: "A magnificent new Sporting Car . . . coach-built body fully sprung, ball-bearing back axle, opening side door, windscreen, dummy hood and lamps, Dunlop pneumatic tyres on tangent-spoked wheels, all bright parts chromium-plated . . .". In addition to these features, note the hand-brake (its knobbed lever visible in the photograph) and the well-modelled radiator surmounted by a mascot. The spare wheel is non-original. Length: 53in (135cm).*

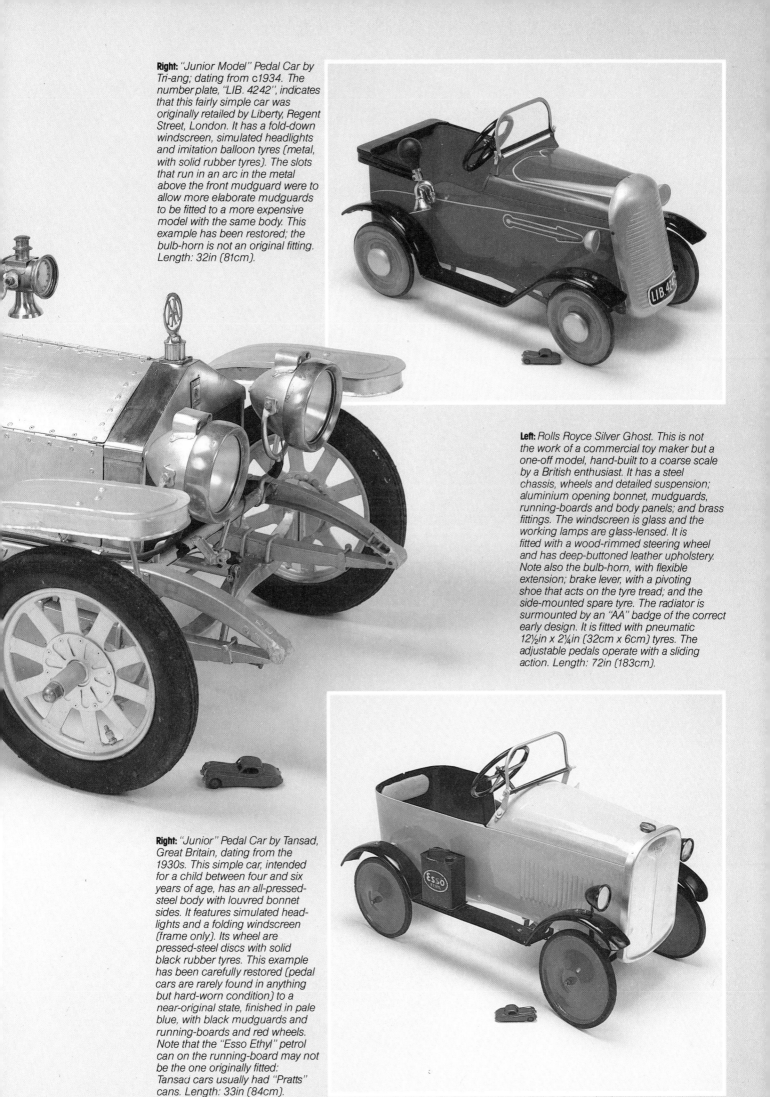

Right: *"Junior Model" Pedal Car by Tri-ang; dating from c1934. The number plate, "LIB. 4242", indicates that this fairly simple car was originally retailed by Liberty, Regent Street, London. It has a fold-down windscreen, simulated headlights and imitation balloon tyres (metal, with solid rubber tyres). The slots that run in an arc in the metal above the front mudguard were to allow more elaborate mudguards to be fitted to a more expensive model with the same body. This example has been restored; the bulb-horn is not an original fitting. Length: 32in (81cm).*

Left: *Rolls Royce Silver Ghost. This is not the work of a commercial toy maker but a one-off model, hand-built to a coarse scale by a British enthusiast. It has a steel chassis, wheels and detailed suspension; aluminium opening bonnet, mudguards, running-boards and body panels; and brass fittings. The windscreen is glass and the working lamps are glass-lensed. It is fitted with a wood-rimmed steering wheel and has deep-buttoned leather upholstery. Note also the bulb-horn, with flexible extension; brake lever, with a pivoting shoe that acts on the tyre tread; and the side-mounted spare tyre. The radiator is surmounted by an "AA" badge of the correct early design. It is fitted with pneumatic 12½in x 2¼in (32cm x 6cm) tyres. The adjustable pedals operate with a sliding action. Length: 72in (183cm).*

Right: *"Junior" Pedal Car by Tansad, Great Britain, dating from the 1930s. This simple car, intended for a child between four and six years of age, has an all-pressed-steel body with louvred bonnet sides. It features simulated head-lights and a folding windscreen (frame only). Its wheel are pressed-steel discs with solid black rubber tyres. This example has been carefully restored (pedal cars are rarely found in anything but hard-worn condition) to a near-original state, finished in pale blue, with black mudguards and running-boards and red wheels. Note that the "Esso Ethyl" petrol can on the running-board may not be the one originally fitted: Tansad cars usually had "Pratts" cans. Length: 33in (84cm).*

Above: "Bugatti" Powered Car; a one-off model built by a British enthusiast in the 1970s. This two-seater is powered by a single-cylinder petrol engine with a lawn-mower type pull-start (visible on the bonnet side) and has forward and reverse gears. The body is aluminium and the radiator has a brass surround and a steel-mesh grille. It has a fold-down windscreen, a faired rear-view mirror, PVC-upholstered seats and simulated filler caps. It is fitted with cable-operated Ackerman-type steering, wire-spoked wheels with pneumatic tyres and cantilever front springing. Length: 72in (183cm).

Right: "Comet" Pedal Car by Tri-ang (Lines Brother Ltd), Great Britain; dating from the early 1930s. This simple single-seater for a young child was one of the cheapest pedal cars in Tri-ang's range: it was priced at 17s 11d (89½p, $1.07) in 1931. It has a pressed-steel radiator, bonnet and seat-back, and a wooden chassis, seat and steering-wheel rim. Its metal disc wheels have wired-on rubber tyres of narrow section. Note the number plate, "LB 3067": the "LB" stands for "Lines Brothers". Length: 33in (84cm).

Right: *"De Dion" Pedal Car by Tri-ang (Lines Brothers Ltd), Great Britain; dating from the 1960s. This "vintage" car has a pressed-steel body; a tubular metal chassis with a sprung rear axle; plastic mud-guards, steering-wheel and side-lamps; and a plastic-upholstered, wooden-backed seat. The starting-handle mounted in the front of the chassis incorporates a "clicker" mechanism, and the wire-spoked wheels are fitted with moulded rubber tyres. Length: 36in (91cm).*

Right: *"Triumph Dolomite" Pedal Car by Leeway, Great Britain; dating from the early 1950s. Although the modelling of its chrome-plated radiator certainly marks this car as a representation of a Triumph Dolomite, it was catalogued by Leeway simply as "Model 16/11". It has an all-steel body with an opening door, and is fitted with a mascot, dummy head- and sidelights, and pressed-steel balloon-type wheels with moulded rubber tyres. The bulb-horn is a non-original item. Length: 45in (114cm).*

113

Above: *Austin Pathfinder Special Pedal Racing Car by Austin Motors, Great Britain; dating from the late 1940s.* "Based on the famous Austin Seven O.H.V. Racing Car which won numerous awards in British track and road events before the war, the Pathfinder Special is a model to delight the heart of every boy. Safe, comfortable and easily handled, this little car will be a treasured possession for many happy years": so claimed the maker's catalogue issued in 1949. This is, indeed, an extremely well-constructed and attractive toy, with a pressed-steel body brilliantly finished in red. The radiator and rear bumpers are chromed, and the bonnet, secured by a leather strap, opens to show a dummy O.H.V. engine complete with sparking plugs and leads. The seat is felt-padded and upholstered in leather-cloth. The treadle drive, acting on the right-hand rear wheel, is through pedals adjustable for leg-reach. A three-position handbrake is fitted. The pressed-steel hubs revolve on roller-bearings, and the pressed-steel wheels are fitted with 12½in x 2¼in (32cm x 6cm) Dunlop pneumatic tyres. Length: 63in (160cm).

Above: *Single-Seat Pedal Car by an unidentified French maker; almost certainly dating from the early 1930s. Seen in a partially-restored state, and finished in red with details in black, this handsome car has a pressed-steel body with a radiator that is perhaps intended to represent that of a Bugatti. It is fitted with twin exhaust pipes and has an operating exterior-mounted handbrake. Its crank drive operates on the right-hand rear wheel. The five-spoked wheels are of cast alloy and are fitted with solid tyres of smooth rubber. Length: 51in (130cm).*

Below: *"Brooklands No 8" Pedal Racing Car ("De Luxe" Model) by Tri-ang (Lines Brothers Ltd), Great Britain; dating from the 1930s. This example of a toy that is now quite hard to find has been restored: the aluminium body and radiator were originally polished bright, but the red enamelling of the chassis and wheel rims is in accordance with the original finish. The bulb horn (and, of course, the "Michelin Man" driver!) are later additions. The spoked wheels are fitted with 12½in x 2¼in (32cm x 6cm) Dunlop Cord pneumatic tyres. Length: 55in (140cm).*

Left: *Single-Seat Pedal Racing Car of British make; dating from the late 1940s. This is not the work of a commercial toymaker, but a one-off model built by a British aircraft engineer (and recently restored to its most attractive finish in British racing green). It is robustly constructed, with a body of beaten aluminium, incorporating bonnet louvres and a raised head-rest fairing, and a well-detailed plated radiator grille and bumpers. It is fitted with crank drive working on the rear wheels and has an operating handbrake. The two-piece wheels are of pressed steel secured by five bolts (note the eared knock-off hub nuts) and are fitted with pneumatic tyres. It is an extremely free-running car with a fine performance. Length: 62in (157cm).*

Right: *Atco Trainer Two-Seater Car* by Atco (Austin Motor Company), Great Britain; dating from the 1930s. This most interesting vehicle falls into a category somewhere between that of a toy and an educational aid, since it was marketed as a training aid for young drivers. One may conclude, however, that its true function will have been that of a fascinating and expensive plaything, since even in the more spacious 1930s it is hardly likely to have been used on the road by a juvenile driver. The car is powered by a single-cylinder petrol engine mounted at the rear (the lid of the engine compartment is shown open), which is started by a lever (clearly seen in the photograph) set in the centre of the PVC-upholstered bench seat. Note the gear lever set to the driver's right and the exterior-mounted handbrake. Ackerman steering is fitted. The body is of pressed steel, with bright steel bumpers at front and rear and a bright radiator grille. Bicycle-type

mudguards are fitted over the split-rim wheels with their pneumatic treaded tyres. This example has undergone some restoration and is now finished in dark green, with a modified Austin "Flying A" bonnet mascot and the maker's name and a Royal Warrant badge on the bonnet side. Length: 72in (183cm).

Above: *"Bugatti" Pedal Racing Car* by Eureka, France; dating from the early 1930s: the front axle is stamped "12/32", probably signifying that the car was made, or its design registered, in December 1932. The example shown was the cheapest and simplest in the French maker's "Bugatti" series. It has a well-modelled radiator, a pressed-steel body incorporating two sets of horizontal louvres on either side of the bonnet, and pressed-steel wheels with solid rubber tyres that bear a moulded tread pattern. This example has been restored, but only the bulb-horn is non-original. Eureka produced its "Bugatti" in a larger "touring" version, with the addition of bumpers, lights and a side-mounted spare wheel; and in a still larger version, with an opening bonnet, perforated disc wheels fitted with pneumatic tyres, and a freewheel mechanism incorporated into its pedal drive. Length: 33in (84cm).

Above: *"Argyle" Pedal Car* by Tansad, Great Britain; dating from the early 1930s. Seen here in partially restored condition, but in its original red finish with printed yellow louvres and bonnet trim, this single-seat car has an all-pressed-steel body and a radiator with a printed grille. It is fitted with an opening door, a windscreen that folds down, and a padded seat-back. The dashboard bears a fine array of printed instrument dials. The metal disc wheels are fitted with solid rubber tyres that retain traces of a moulded tread pattern. The rear of the car bears a contemporary "National Road Safety Campaign" transfer. Although of the correct period type, the "Red-X" petrol can mounted on the running-board is not the one originally fitted: Tansad cars with this feature usually had "Pratts" petrol cans (and, it may be noted, Tri-ang cars of the same period usually had "Shell" cans). Length: 33.5in (85cm).

Left: *"Buick Regal" Pedal Car* by Tri-ang (Lines Brothers Ltd), Great Britain; dating from around 1931. This is a toy of extremely good quality and it is shown here in excellent original condition, having undergone no restoration. (It is worth noting here that the general opinion among collectors seems to be that the value of a toy that has been professionally restored to near-original condition may be around 70-75 per cent of the value of an unrestored item in very good condition.) This car has a pressed-steel, single-seat body, incorporating bonnet fairings and louvres, tubular steel front bumpers, and a well-modelled radiator with a chromed frame, surmounted by a cast metal mascot. It is fitted with working, battery-powered headlights and sidelights (with an on/off switch mounted on the dashboard) and has an opening door with a cast handle. Other details visible in the photograph include a front number plate, an imitation "road tax disc" in a holder mounted just below the near-side sidelight, a fold-down windshield with a chromed frame and a clear perspex screen, a rear-view mirror, and a simulated folded hood. The dashboard bears a well-printed array of instrument panels. Its wire-spoked wheels are fitted with treaded tyres of solid rubber, and it has a suspension system with half-elliptic springing. A detachable boot with a luggage rack was originally bolted on at the rear, but is now missing. Length: 43in (109cm).

Left: *"Bullnose Morris" Pedal Car by Tri-ang (Lines Brothers Ltd), Great Britain; dating from the 1920s.* With a metal frame and wooden panels, this most attractive representation of a famous British-built touring car has a bicycle-type chain drive. It is fitted with a sprung front bumper, front and rear number plates and a rear luggage rack. Other features include a well-modelled radiator (with Lines Brothers' punning trademark impressed on its crown) surmounted by a realistic filler cap and temperature gauge, an opening door with a chromed handle, a wood-rimmed steering wheel and an adjustable seat. It is fitted with a battery-powered buzzer that simulates a starter-motor. The fold-down windscreen that was originally provided is missing from this otherwise excellent example. The detachable disc wheels are fitted with solid rubber tyres. This high-quality toy was advertised in 1927 at a price of £5 5s 0d (£5.25, $6.30), which was then more than the weekly wage of the average British worker; one of the more expensive items in Tri-ang's range. Length: 49in (124·5cm).

Right: *"Frazer Nash" Pedal Racing Car* by Tri-ang, Great Britain; dating from c1934. It has a pressed-steel body on a tubular steel chassis with quarter-elliptic leaf springing. The wire-spoked wheels are fitted with Dunlop Cord pneumatic tyres. This unrestored car bears no trademark: it is possibly a modification of the Tri-ang M.G. pedal car. Length: 59in (150cm).

Left: *"Bimbo Racer" Electric-Powered Sports Car* by Sila, Italy; dating from around 1956. Modelled on a Ferrari V-12 sports car of the period, this left-hand drive, two-seater play car has a fibreglass body, incorporating an air intake on the bonnet, and is finished in Italian racing red. A battery-powered electric motor drives one rear wheel, giving a maximum speed of around 4-5mph (6-8km/h). It has working headlights, with chromed rims, and an electric horn. The radiator grille is made of perforated metal mesh and the seats are upholstered in blue leatherette. The well-modelled, chromed disc wheels, with simulated spokes, are held in place by eared nuts and are fitted with 12½in x 2¼in (32cm x 6cm) pneumatic treaded tyres. This example of a luxury toy has undergone restoration, and still awaits the fitting of a clear plastic windscreen like that originally featured. Length: 66in (168cm).

Right: *"Pilgrim Special" Pedal Car* by an unidentified Australian maker; dating from around 1960. Possibly modelled on an indigenous Holden car, this small and fairly basic single-seater for a young child is constructed of simple heavy-gauge steel body pressings, spot-welded together. Steel bumpers are fitted front and rear. Printed details include the radiator grille, the model's name and manufacturer's trademark on the bonnet, wing motifs at front and rear, and a side trim of stars and stripes. It has a wire windscreen (frame only) and plated brightwork headlights. Crank drive transmits power to one rear wheel. The pressed-steel disc wheels have chromed hubcaps and are fitted with solid tyres of smooth rubber. Length: 38in (97cm).

Right: *Triumph T.R.3A Pedal Car by an unidentified British maker; dating from the late 1950s. This well-proportioned representation of a famous British sports car of the period, with twin bucket-seats, has a body of moulded fibreglass. It is finished in red, with applied chromed brightwork "Triumph" lettering, surmounted by an enamelled "Triumph" badge, above the radiator; note also the enamelled Union Jack badge applied to the radiator grille. Other brightwork details include front bumpers, a* well-modelled radiator grille, headlight frames, bonnet and boot catches, and rear filler cap. Indicators with coloured plastic lenses are set into the radiator grille, and the working headlights (the bulb missing from the right-hand light in this example) are battery-powered. The wire-spoked, chromium-plated wheels are fitted with 12½in x 2¼in (32cm x 6cm) pneumatic tyres. This example of a toy of good quality is in the process of restoration to its original condition. Length: 72in (183cm).*

Left: *Pedal Racing Car by an unidentified maker (almost certainly of French manufacture); dating from the early 1960s. Finished in blue, it is a fairly simple single-seat car and is apparently modelled on a Talbot-Lago racing car of the period; yet another example of toymakers' faith in the appeal of racing cars to their juvenile customers. It has a body of pressed steel, incorporating basic detail and with two rows of louvres applied on either side of the bonnet. The spoked steering wheel is also of steel. A radiator grille of wire mesh constitutes the only other detail. The metal disc wheels have chromium-plated hubcaps and are fitted with treaded tyres of solid rubber. Length: 56·5in (143·5cm).*

Above: *"Ford Zephyr" Pedal Car by Tri-ang (Lines Brothers Ltd), Great Britain; dating from the early 1950s. Finished in blue, this is a fairly well-detailed toy, with an all-metal body and plated bright-work bumpers (with an applied "AA" badge on the front bumper), a boldly-modelled radiator, headlight frames (with battery-powered head-lights), bonnet trim strip, windscreen frame and hubcaps. A dummy gear-shift lever is mounted on the steering column. It has an exterior-mounted handbrake and its red-rimmed metal wheels are fitted with tyres of solid rubber. Length: 48in (122cm).*

Right: *Pedal Racing Car by Geordownin, Great Britain; dating from around 1930—and making an interesting comparison with the very similar toy of the 1960s, shown left. Seen here in its original red finish, it is considerably "play-worn": this is usual with pedal cars, which were intended for active play, took hard knocks, and more often than not will require restoration. It is a simple single-seater with a boat-tailed body of pressed steel. It is fitted with crank drive (the transmission to the rear axle is just visible in the photograph) and has a simple steering system with a front axle that is pivoted at the centre. It has large disc wheels fitted with narrow tyres of solid rubber. Length: 46·5in (118cm).*

Right: *Triumph T.R.7. Pedal Car by Hamilton Brooks & Company, Great Britain; dating from the late 1970s. It is finished in cream, with black trim, an applied "Triumph" emblem on the bonnet, and the number plate "HB 2". This handsome toy, extremely well-finished and with seats upholstered in tartan cloth, has a moulded plastic body, incorporating louvres and simulated "pop-up" headlights, and black moulded plastic bumpers front and rear. Note the coloured plastic indicator lenses set into the bumpers. It has battery-powered working headlights (set beneath the bumpers) and rearlights, and an electrically-powered horn. The windscreen frame is black plastic; the screen itself is clear perspex. The well-modelled plastic wheels are fitted with pneumatic treaded rubber tyres. A Union Jack sticker on the windscreen (stemming from a "Buy British" campaign of the time) proclaims "I've Got British Parts"—and suggests, therefore, that it is at least in part of non-British make. Length: 69in (175cm).*

Left: *"Ferrari" Pedal Racing Car by an unidentified British maker—but thought to be the work of Tri-ang (Lines Brother Ltd)—dating from the late 1950s or early 1960s. The positioning of the chromium-plated exhaust pipe along the side suggests that this racing car is modelled on a front-engined Ferrari of the late 1950s. Note the applied Ferrari badge just forward of the cockpit. The metal wheels, with simulated wire spokes and "knock-off" hubcaps, are fitted with untreaded tyres of solid rubber. The radiator grille that was originally fitted is missing from this example, which, unlike a number of the other pedal cars shown in this book, had not yet undergone restoration by its present owner. Length: 44in (112cm).*

Right: *"Vanwall" Pedal Racing Car by Tri-ang (Lines Brothers Ltd), Great Britain; dating from the late 1950s. Finished in red, with a bright metal radiator and side-mounted external exhaust pipe, it has an applied Union Jack on its bonnet, as befits a representation of a successful British racing car of the period. The bonnet and chassis are constructed of pressed steel and the perforated pressed-steel wheels, with cleverly-simulated spokes, are fitted with untreaded solid rubber tyres. The three-spoked steering wheel is made of moulded plastic—note the external steering links above the front wheels—and the seat is upholstered in black PVC with white piping. A perspex windscreen is fitted. Length: 45·5in (116cm).*

Top left: *Vauxhall Tourer Pedal Car by Tri-ang, Great Britain; dating from 1936. It has a pressed-steel body with an opening side-door and a well-modelled Vauxhall-style bonnet and radiator. The 8in (20cm). balloon disc wheels are fitted with 0·5in (1·27cm) solid rubber tyres. It was originally equipped with two dummy side lamps and petrol and oil cans; those features are missing from this restored example, which has a non-original bulb-horn. Length: 32in (81cm).*

Centre left: *"Citroën" Pedal Car by Tri-ang (Lines Brothers Ltd), Great Britain; dating from the 1930s. This simple car has a pressed-steel body (note the tubular front and rear bumpers) with an opening side-door. The crank drive to the rear wheels is just visible in the photograph. It has balloon disc wheels with solid rubber tyres. The dummy headlights and number plate originally fitted are missing from this restored example, which has a non-original mascot. Length: 44in (112cm).*

Left: *"Austin J (Junior) Forty" Pedal Car by the Austin Motor Company, Great Britain; some 32,100 of these cars were produced in 1950-71. It is made of sheet steel: surplus metal from Austin's Birmingham works was sent to a purpose-built factory in Wales, where disabled miners built the "Joycars" as part of a rehabilitation programme. It has battery-operated headlights and a bonnet that opens on a detailed engine. Length: 63in (160cm).*

Left: *Rolls Royce Corniche Electric-Powered Car by Shara Triang Ltd, Great Britain; currently in production. This luxury toy has a moulded plastic body with plated brightwork details, including a fairly convincing Rolls Royce radiator that is somewhat spoiled by a poor representation of the famous mascot. It has been produced as a pedal car, but the example shown here is driven by an electric motor powered by two 6-volt batteries contained in the boot, giving two forward speeds and reverse. A battery charger is provided, and a further battery powers such accessories as working headlights and sidelights, indicators and hazard warning lights, a horn and a simulated starter motor. It is intended for children of 3-8 years of age. Length: 50in (127cm).*

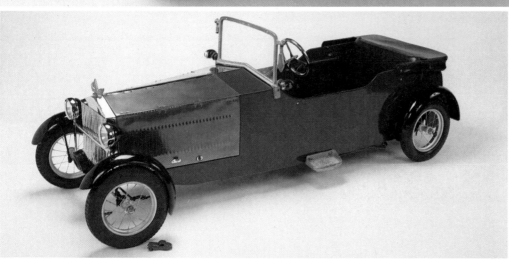

Left: *Rolls Royce Electric-Powered Car by Tri-ang, Great Britain; dating from the early 1930s. This fine toy (here seen restored to near-original condition) is driven by a Lucas 12-volt electric motor on the rear axle, powered by two 6-volt batteries fitted beneath the bonnet. It was claimed to have a maximum endurance, before recharging was needed, of 12-15 miles (19-24km) at 5mph (8km/h). The power is controlled by a foot pedal and a three-position (forward, neutral, reverse) gear lever. A hand-brake acts on the rear axle. The finely-modelled radiator is chrome-plated, as are the working headlights, side-lights and rearlights. The opening bonnet, of bright metal, has louvres on either side; the body panels are wood. Length: 80in (203cm).*

125

Index

A

American, unidentified
  Roadster, 39
Arnold, 22
  Mercedes-Benz Remote-Control
    Sedan, 44
  Remote-Control Car, box, 35
  Remote-Control Convertible, 44
Asahi
  Rolls Royce Camargue, 81
Atco see Austin Motors
Austin-Motors
  Atco Trainer Two-Seater Car, 116
  "Austin J (Junior) Forty" Pedal Car,
    124
  Austin Pathfinder Special Pedal
    Racing Car, 114
Australian, unidentified
  "Pilgrim Special" Racing Car, 119

B

Bandai
  Buick Convertible, 42
  Cadillac Gear Shift Car, 42
    box, 34
  Chevrolet Convertible, 42
  Chevrolet Station Wagon, 43
  Chrysler Imperial Convertible, 42
    box, 34
  Corvair Bertone, 84
  Ferrari Gear Shift Car, 86
    box, 34
  Ford Thunderbird, 43
  Pontiac Convertible, 43
Bing
  Open Tourer, 38-39
  Saloon Car, 38
Brimtoy
  Open Tourer, 38
British, unidentified
  "Ferrari" Pedal Racing Car, 122
  Ford Zephyr Saloon with Caravan, 15
  Triumph T.R.3A Pedal Car, 120
Bub, Karl, 21
  Open Tourer, 39
Burnett Ltd, 22

C

Chinese, unidentified
  Sedan-convertible, 40
  Streamline Electric Sedan, 44
CIJ
  Alfa Romeo P2 Racing Car, 8
  Renault Dauphinoise box, 37
  Renault Fregate box, 37
Citroën, 21
Compagnie Industrielle du Jouet see
  CIJ
Conrad Modell
  Audi Quattro, 77
  Mercedes-Benz 190/190E
    Saloon, 76
  Mercedes-Benz 240TD/300TD/
    230T/250T/280TE Estate Car, 76
  Volkswagen Passat GLS, 76
  Volkswagen Passat Variant GLS, 76
  Volkswagen Santana GL, 77
  Volkswagen Scirocco GLi, 76
Corgi Toys, 26-27
  Aston Martin DB4, 94
  Austin A60 Motor School Car, 27
  Austin Healey 100-4, 93
  Bentley T Series, 81
  B.R.M. Racing Car, 93
  catalogue, 33
  Citroën "Le Dandy" Coupé, 65
  Cooper Maserati, 87
  Cooper Maserati, Racing Car, 86-87
  Ford Consul, 60
  Jaguar "E" Type, 93
  Lotus Climax Racing Car, 87
  M.G.B. GT, 93
  M.G.C. GT, 92-93
  Riley Pathfinder, 60
  Rolls Royce 1912 Silver Ghost, 80
  Rolls Royce Corniche, 81
  Vanwall Racing Car, 93
  Volkswagen 1500 Karmann Ghia, 64
  Volvo P1800, 27
Crescent Toys
  Aston Martin D.B.3S 2.9-Litre Sports
    Racing Car, 90
  B.R.M. Mark II Grand Prix Car, 90
  Connaught 2-Litre Grand Prix Car, 90
  Cooper Bristol 2-Litre Grand Prix
    Car, 90

Ferrari 2.5-Litre Grand Prix Car, 90
Gordini 2.5-Litre Grand Prix Car, 90
Maserati 2.5-Litre Grand Prix
  Car, 90
Mercedes-Benz 2.5-Litre Grand Prix
  Car, 90
Vanwall 2.5-Litre Grand Prix Car, 90
Cursor Modell
  Mercedes-Benz Gelandewagen
    240GD/230G/300GD/280GE, 76

D

Dalia Solido
  Alfa Romeo Guilia T2, 94
  Aston Martin 3L, 95
  DB Panhard Le Mans, 94-95
  Ferrari 2.5-Litre, 95
  Ferrari Type 500 TRC, 95
  Fiat Abarth 1000, 94
  Porsche GT Le Mans, 94
  Porsche Spyder, 95
Dinky Toys, 24-25
  A.C. Aceca Coupé box, 37
  Alfa Romeo 33, 103
  Alfa Romeo 1900 Super Sprint,
    60-61, 73
  Alfa Romeo 1900 Super Sprint
    Coupé, 64
  Alfa Romeo Racing Car, 91
  Alvis Sports Tourer, 50
  Ambulances, 46
  Armstrong-Siddeley Coupé, 50
  Armstrong-Siddeley Limousine, 46
  Aston Martin DB3 Sport, box, 37
  Aston Martin DB3S (Competition
    Finish), 51
  Aston Martin DB5 Volante, 21
  Aston Martin DB6, 21
  Austin 7 Saloon, 46-47
  Austin 7 Tourer, 47
  Austin A90 Atlantic, 51
  Austin A105, 58
  Austin Devon Saloon, 54
  Austin Healey 100 (Competition
    Finish), 51
  Austin Healey 100 (Touring Finish),
    103
  Austin Healey Sprite Mark II, 93

Austin Somerset, 55
Auto Union Racing Car, 86
Bentley Two-Seater Sports Coupé, 48
B.E.V. Truck, 7
Borgward Isabella, 65
British Salmson (Two-Seater
  Sports), 49
Buick Roadmaster, 66-67
Buick Viceroy Saloon Car, 52
Cadillac 62, 57
Cadillac Eldorado, 57
catalogues, 32-33
Chevrolet Corvair, 66
Chrysler 1308 GT (Alpine), 71
Chrysler "Airflow" Saloon, 46
Chrysler New Yorker Convertible, 67
Chrysler Royal Sedan, 52-53
Chrysler Saratoga, 67
Citroën 2CV, 70
  (1950 Model), 63
Citroën 3CV, 64
Citroën 11BL, 63
Citroën CX Pallas, 70
Citroën DS19, 63
Citroën DS19 (1955 Model), 64
Citroën DS23, 70
Citroën Dyane, 70
Citroën Presidentielle, 23
Cooper Bristol Racing Car, 91
Daf Saloon, 65
Daimler, 46
Daimler V8 2.5-Litre, 59
De Soto 59 Diplomat, 66
Dino Ferrari, 75
Dodge Royal Sedan, 56
Estate Car, 53
Ferrari 250 GT, 72
Ferrari 275 GTB, 72
Ferrari 312P, 102
Ferrari P5, 75
Ferrari Racing Car, 90, 91
Fiat 600, 69
Fiat 1200 Grande Vue, 69
Fiat 1800 Estate Car, 69
Fiat 2000 Station Wagon, 61
Fiat Abarth 2000 Pininfarina, 74
Fiat (2-Seater) Saloon, 47
Ford Capri, 58, 78
Ford Capri Rally Car box, 37
Ford Consul Corsair, 58
Ford Corsair 2000E, 61

Ford Cortina, 58
Ford Cortina Rally Car, 61
Ford Escort, 61
Ford Fairlane, 57
Ford Fiesta, 71
Ford Fordor Sedan, 53
Ford Galaxie 500, 66
Ford Mercury Cougar, 57
Ford Mustang, 61
Ford Thunderbird Convertible, 66
Ford Thunderbird Coupé, 66
Ford Vedette (1949 Model), 62
Ford Vedette (1953 Model), 62
Ford Zephyr, 60
Frazer-Nash B.M.W. Sports Car,
  50-51
Grand Sport (2-Seater), 37
Grand Sport (4-Seater), 47
Grand Sport Coupé, 47
Hillman Imp, 58
Hillman Minx, 58, 60
Hillman Minx Saloon, 55
Holden Special Sedan, 24
Hudson Commodore Sedan, 53
Hudson Hornet, 56
Humber Hawk, 60
Humber Vogue, 49
H.W.M. Racing Car, 90
Jaguar 3.4-Litre Mark II, 60
Jaguar "E" Type, 24
Jaguar Mark 10, 61
Jaguar Sports Car, 51
Jaguar XK120, 7, 55
Lagonda Sports Coupé, 21, 50
Limousine, 47
Lincoln Continental, 56, 61
Lincoln Premier, 66
Lincoln Zephyr Coupé, 52
Maserati Racing Car, 91
Maserati Sports Car, 96
Matra Simca Bagheera, 70
Matra Sports M530, 74-75
Matra V12 F1, 87
McLaren M8A Can-Am, 102
Mercedes-Benz 190SL, 65
Mercedes-Benz 230SL, 65
Mercedes-Benz 300SE, 65
Mercedes-Benz C111, 74, 75
Mercedes-Benz Racing Car, 86
M.G. Midget (Competition Finish), 51
M.G. Midget (Touring Finish), 51

M.G. Sports Car, 92
M.G.B., box, 37
Monteverdi 375L, 75
Morris Oxford Saloon, 55
Nash Rambler, 56
Oldsmobile Six Sedan Car, 52
Opel Admiral, 69
Opel Ascona, 71
Opel Commodore, 61
Opel Kadett Saloon, 69
Opel Kapitan, 59
Opel Rekord, 69
  box, 37
Opel Rekord 1900 Coupé, 75
Packard Clipper, 56
Packard Convertible, 56
Packard Super 8 Touring Sedan, 52
Panhard 24, 69
Panhard PL17 Saloon, 62
Peugeot Car, 47
Peugeot 203 Sedan, 62
Peugeot 204, 71
Peugeot 204 Cabriolet, 69
Peugeot 204 Saloon, 65
Peugeot 304, 71
Peugeot 403 Saloon, 62
Peugeot 403 UF Estate Car, 62
Peugeot 404, 58, 69
Peugeot 404 Pininfarina, 68-69
Peugeot 404 Saloon, 64
Peugeot 404 Shooting Brake, 65, 69
Peugeot 504, 71, 75
Peugeot 504 Cabriolet, 64
Plymouth Belvedere Coupé, 67
Plymouth Fury Sports, 61
Porsche Carrera 6, 74
Racing Cars, 23, 86
Rambler Cross-Country Station
  Wagon, 56-57
Renault 4L, 70
Renault 4L "Depannage Autoroutes",
  68
Renault 4L "P&T", 68
Renault 6, 68, 70
Renault 12, 71
Renault 12 Gordini, 68
Renault 14, 71
Renault 17TS, 70
Renault Dauphine, 63
Renault Floride Coupé, 63
Renault R8 Gordini, 68

Renault R16, 71
Renault R16 TX, 71
Riley Saloon, 54
Rolls Royce, 47
Rolls Royce Phantom V, 80-81
Rolls Royce Silver Wraith, 81
Rover Saloon, 47
Rover 75 Saloon, 55
Simca 1000, 69
Simca 1100, 70-71
Simca 1500 GLS Shooting Brake, 68
Simca Aronde, 62
Simca 9 Aronde, 62-63
Simca Chambord, 63
Simca Versailles, 63
Singer Gazelle, 60
Singer Vogue, 60
Sports Cars, 23
Standard Vanguard Saloon, 54-55
Studebaker Commander Coupé, 66
Studebaker Golden Hawk, 57
Studebaker Land Cruiser, 53
Studebaker President, 57
Studebaker State Commander
    Saloon Car, 53
Sunbeam Alpine (Competition
    Finish), 51
Sunbeam Rapier, 60
Sunbeam Talbot Sports, 50
Super Streamline Saloon, 47
Surtees TS5, 87
Talbot-Lago Racing Car, 91
Triumph 1300, 58-59
Triumph 1800 Saloon, 54
Triumph 2000, 58
Triumph T.R.2 (Competition Finish),
    51
Triumph Vitesse, 58
Vauxhall, 46
Vauxhall Cresta, 59
Vauxhall Victor Estate Car, 59
Vauxhall Viva, 59
Vogue Saloon, 47
Volkswagen, 59
Volkswagen 1300 Sedan, 75
Volkswagen 1500, 59
Volkswagen Karmann Ghia Coupé,
    59, 64
Volkswagen Scirocco, 70
Volvo 122S, 59
Volvo 1800 S, 75

Durago
    Opel Ascona 400 Rally Car, 79
    Rolls Royce Camargue, 80
    Rolls Royce Silver Shadow II, 80

E

"Empire Made", unidentified
    Jaguar XK150, 45
Erti
    "General Lee" Car, 78
Eureka
    "Bugatti" Pedal Racing Car, 116
European, unidentified
    Rear-Entrance Tonneau Car, 38

F

Faracars
    Indianapolis S.T.P. Turbine Car, 87
Fischer, H. & Co.
    Taxi, 39
French, unidentified
    Pedal Racing Car, 120
    Single Seat Pedal Racing Car, 115

G

"G"
    Porsche 930 Turbo, 79
Gama
    B.M.W. M1, 77
    Ferrari Open Sports Car, 96
    Ford GT40, 97
    Ford Taunus 17M Station Wagon, 15
    Opel Ascona, 77
    Racing Car box, 37
    Shell Filling Station, 30
Geordownin
    Pedal Racing Car, 121
German, unidentified
    Shell Filling Station, 30
    Station Wagon, 40
Guntermann, 21

H

"H"
    New Ford Sedan, 42
Haji
    New Edsel, 42
Hamilton Brooks & Co.
    Triumph T.R.7 Pedal Car, 122
Handbuilt
    "Bugatti" Powered Car, 112
    Rolls Royce Silver Ghost Pedal Car,
        111
    Single-Seat Pedal Car, 115
Hauser, 22
Husky Models catalogue, 32

I

Ichiko
    Plymouth Sedan, 42-43
    box, 35
Intercars
    Ferrari Dino, 94
Italian, unidentified
    Cisitalia Model 202 box, 36
Ites
    Jeep, 45

J

Japanese, unidentified
    Cadillac Sedan, 41
    Convertible, 41
    "Fairlane 500" Sedan, 43
    Hadtop, 41
    New World Car, 41
    Novelty Veteran car, 10
    Saloon Car, 40-41
    Sedan, 41
JEP, 21
    Hispano Suiza Touring Car, 7
JNF
    Racing Car, 84-85
    box, 35
    Silver Arrow Racing Car, 85
    box, 35

Jouets en Paris see JEP
Joustra
    Racing Car, 85

K

"K"
    Three Assorted Cars, 45
Kingsbury, 21
KKK
    Station Wagon, 40
Koh-I-Noor Hardmuth see Ites
"KY"
    Convertible, 44-45

L

Leeway
    "Triumph Dolomite" Pedal Car, 113
Lesney Products Ltd, 28
    1929 4.5-Litre Bentley, 28
    1929 Bentley Le Mans, 27
    1910 Benz Limousine, 82
    1923 Type 35 Bugatti, 28
    1913 Cadillac, 82
    catalogue, 32
    1911 Daimler, 83
    1911 Maxwell Roadster, 83
    1908 Mercedes Grand Prix, 27
    1913 Mercer Raceabout, 28
    1911 Model "T" Ford, 82
    1926 Morris Cowley "Bullnose", 27
    1909 Opel Coupé, 82
    1912 Packard Landaulet, 83
    1930 Packard Victoria, 83
    1907 Peugeot, 82
    1914 Prince Henry Vauxhall, 82
    1912 Rolls Royce, 82
    1906 Rolls Royce "Silver Ghost", 83
    1907 Rolls Royce "Silver Ghost", 28
    1912 Simplex, 82-83
    1904 Spyker, 83
    1914 Stutz, 82
    1909 Thomas Flyabout, 83
Lincoln International
    Cadillac Convertible, 17
    Ford Thunderbird Convertible, 17

Mercedes-Benz 300SL, 17
MGA Sports Roadster, 45
Remote-Control Jaguar Car, 10
Lineol, 22
Lines Brothers Ltd see Tri-ang

M

Mamod
    Steam Roadster, 13
Manoil, 23
Mansei Toy Company see Haji
Märklin, 22
    Ferrari box, 36
    Porsche 907, 102
    Porsche 910, 102
Marx
    "Marx-Mobile" Electric-Powered Toy
        Car, 123
Matchbox see Lesney
Mebetoys
    Abarth 3000PS, 105
    Alfa Romeo 33-3, 105
    Alfa Romeo Duetta Spyder box, 36
    Ferrari 313PB, 103
    Ferrari 365 GTC-4, 74
    Ferrari Can-Am, 105
    Ford Mark II, 97
    Ford Mustang Boss 302, 97
    Lamborghini Urraco, 74
    Lola T212, 102
    McLaren M8D, 102-3
    Maserati Bora, 74
    Toyota 2000GT, 74
Meccano, 22, 23-24
    see also Dinky Toys
Meier/Kohnstam, J.Ph.
    "Penny Toys" Limousine, 39
    Taxi, 39
Mercury
    Alfa Romeo 33, 97
    Alfa Romeo Alfette 158 Racing
        Car, 88
    Alfa Romeo Giulia box, 36
    Alfa Romeo Giulia TZ, 72
    Alfa Romeo Rally Car box, 37
    catalogue, 32
    Chaparral Can-Am 2J, 102
    Cisitalia 1100 Racing Car, 88

Cisitalia 1500 Grand Prix Racing
    Car, 89
Dino Sport, 95
Ferrari 250 LM, 72
    box, 36
Ferrari 330 P2, 94
Ferrari 330 P4, 96
Ferrari 1500 Racing Car, 88-89
Ferrari P312, 96, 103
Ferrari Racing Sports Car, 95
Ferrari Supersqualo, 93
Fiat Abarth 1000 Bialbero, 94
Lancia D24, 96
Lancia D.50 Grand Prix Racing
    Car, 93
Lancia Flavia Coupé, 72
Maserati 3500 GT, 96
Maserati Grand Prix Racing Car, 88
Maserati Racing Car, 88
Mercedes-Benz 196 Grand Prix
    Racing Car, 93
Mercedes-Benz 196 Grand Prix
    Racing Car (Streamlined), 93
Mercedes-Benz 1500 Racing Car, 88
Porsche 908/03, 97, 103
Porsche 917, 96, 107
Porsche Carrera 6 box, 36
Porsche Carrera G, 96, 107
S.V.A. Racing Car, 88
Mini Cars (Anguplas)
    catalogue, 32
Models of Yesteryear see Lesney
Modern Toys see MT
Motorway Models
    MGA Hardtop Sports Saloon, 45
"MT"
    "Three-Style Car", 43

N

Nomura Toys see T.N.
Norev
    Fiat 2300 Coupé, 64
    Matra Sports F2, 86
    Peugeot 204 Coupé, 64-65
N.Z.G.Modell
    Mercedes-Benz 280S/SE/SEL, 76
    Mercedes-Benz 380SEC/500SEC
        Coupé, 76

P

Pilen
Chevrolet Sport (Corvette Stingray) box, 37

Polistil
B.M.W. 525 Berlina, 78-79
Mercedes-Benz 450SL, 78
Peugeot 504 box, 37
Rolls Royce Silver Cloud III, 81
Volkswagen, 79

Politoys (Polistil)
Abarth 3000, 104
Alfa Romeo 33, 104
Alfa Romeo Giulia SS, 72-73
Alfa Romeo Giulia TZ, 72
Alpine Renault, 104
B.R.M. P154 Can-Am, 104
catalogue, 33
Chaparral 2J Racing Car, 17
Chevron GTB 16, 104-5
Ferrari 250 GT Berlinetta, 72
Ferrari 250 Le Mans Pininfarina, 96
Ferrari 330 GTC, 72
Ferrari 512S, 105
Ferrari Dino Berlinetta, 104
Ford GTJ, 97
Ford Lola GT, 97, 102
Ford Mirage, 104
Ford Mustang 2+2 Bertone box, 36
Ghibli Maserati Ghia, 73
Hownet "TX" Sports Racing Car, 96
Iso Rivolta, 72
Lamborghini 350 GT, 73
Lamborghini Bertone Espada, 73
Lamborghini Islero, 73
Lola 260 Can-Am, 105
Lola Aston Martin, 97
Lola T222 Can-Am, 105
March 717-1 Can-Am, 105
Maserati 3500 GT, 73
Maserati Coupé, 73
Matra Simca Sports 660, 105
Matra Sport 630, 104
McLaren Chevrolet M8F Can-Am, 104
Porsche 904 Carrera GTS, 97
Porsche 912, 73
Porsche 917, 97
Porsche 917 Le Mans, 105

Porsche Audi 917-10 Can-Am, 104
Serenissima, 105

Q

Quiralu
Isetta Velam Voiturette ("Baby Car"), 17

S

Sanshin
MGA 1600 Hardtop, 85

Scamold
Alta Racing Car, 88
E.R.A. Racing Car, 88
Maserati Racing Car, 88

Schreyer and Company see Schuco

Schuco (Schreyer and Company), 22
B.M.W. box, 36
B.M.W. 630CS, 74
catalogue, 32-33
Chaparral 2D box, 36
Fiat Abarth box, 36
Mercedes 350SE, 74
Porsche 924, 74

Shara Triang Ltd
Rolls Royce Corniche Electric-Powered Car, 125

Sila
"Bimbo Racer" Electric-Powered Sports Car, 119

Société d'Exploitation du Jouet Joustra see Joustra

Solido
Alfa Romeo 33/3, 107
Alfa Romeo 2600, 72
Alfa Romeo Alfetta GTV, 108
Alpine F111 Racing Car, 86
Alpine Renault 3L, 103
Aston Martin 3L DBR1 300, 95
Aston Martin DB4, 21
Aston Martin DB5 Vantage, 21
B.M.W. 3.0 CLS, 109
B.M.W. 530, 108
B.M.W. 2002 Turbo, 108
B.M.W. M1, 108

B.R.M. V8 Racing Car, 89
catalogues, 32-33
Chaparral 2D, 103
Chaparral 2F, 103
Cooper 1.5-Litre Racing Car, 89
Ferrari 250 GT 2+2, 72
Ferrari 312 PB, 106
Ferrari 330 P3, 106
Ferrari Daytona box, 36
Ferrari V12 F1, 87
Fiat Abarth 131 Rallye, 109
Ford Capri 2600 RV, 108-9
Ford Escort L, 109
Ford Le Mans, 102
Ford Mark IV, 106
Ford Thunderbird, 56
Ferrari 312P, 107
Ferrari 512M, 107
Ferrari 512S, 107
Ferrari V12 F1, 86
Harvey Aluminium Indianapolis Special, 87
Jaguar Le Mans "D" Type, 95
Lancia Stratos, 108
Ligier JS/3, 106
Lola T70 Mark 3B, 107
Lola T280, 106
Lola Climax V8 F1 Racing Car, 86, 89
Lotus Formula One Racing Car, 89
March Formula One Racing Car, 89
March 707 Can-Am, 106
Maserati Indy, 72
Maserati 250 Racing Car, 89
Matra 650, 102
Matra 670 box, 36
Matra Sports Racing Cars, 18
Matra V8 F1, 87
McLaren M8B Can-Am, 106-7
Opel Kadett Coupé GTE, 108
Peugeot 504 Coupé V6, 108
Porsche 908, 107
Porsche 917, 106
Porsche 917/10 TC Can-Am, 107
Porsche Carrera 6, 103
Porsche F.11 Racing Car, 89
Renault 5 Turbo, 109
Rolls Royce Phantom III (1939 Model), 81
Toyota Celica, 108
Vanwall Formula One Racing Car, 89

Spot On see Tri-ang

SSS International
Mercedes-Benz 220S, 40

Structo, 22

Super Champion
Ferrari 312T Grand Prix Racing Car, 98
Ferrari 512M Sports Racing Car "Filipinetti", 99
Ferrari 512M Sports Racing Car "Francorchamps", 99
Ferrari 512M Sports Racing Car "Gelo Racing Team", 99
Ferrari 512M Sports Racing Car "N.A.R.T.", 99
Ferrari 512M Sports Racing Car "Sunoco", 99
Ligier J.S.5 Grand Prix Racing Car, 98
Lola T70 Mk 3B Sports Racing Car "24 Hours Daytona", 101
Lola T70 Mk 3B Sports Racing Car "1000-Km de Paris", 101
Lola T70 Mk 3B Sports Racing Car "Grand Prix d'Autriche", 101
Lola T70 Mk 3B Sports Racing Car "Monza", 101
Lola T70 Mk 3B Sports Racing Car "Nurburgring", 101
Lola T70 Mk 3B Sports Racing Car "Temporada" (Buenos Aires), 101
Porsche 917 Sports Racing Car "Brands Hatch", 100
Porsche 917 Sports Racing Car "David Piper", 100
Porsche 917 Sports Racing Car "Daytona", 100
Porsche 917 Sports Racing Car "Ecurie Hollandaise", 100
Porsche 917 Sports Racing Car "Hockenheim 70", 101
Porsche 917 Sports Racing Car "Le Mans", 100
Porsche 917 Sports Racing Car "Martini Racing Team" (Kayalami), 100
Porsche 917 Sports Racing Car "Monza", 101
Porsche 917 Sports Racing Car "Temporada", 100
Porsche 917H Le Mans Sports Racing Car "Martini Racing Team", 98

Porsche 917K, 99
Porsche 917K Sports Racing Car "Ecurie Gulf John Wyer", 101
Porsche 917K Sports Racing Car "Le Mans 70", 101
Porsche 917K Sports Racing Car "Martini & Rossi Racing Team" (12-hour Sebring), 100-1
Porsche 917K Sports Racing Car "Nurburgring", 101
Porsche 917L Le Mans Sports Racing Car "Ecurie Gulf John Wyer", 98
Porsche 917L Le Mans Sports Racing Car "Essais Lemans", 99
Porsche 917L Le Mans Sports Racing Car "International Martini Racing Team", 98-99
Porsche 917L Le Mans Sports Racing Car "Le Mans 70", 99
Tyrrell P34-2 Grand Prix Racing Car, 98

T

Taguchi
Limousine Car, 41

Taiyo
Assorted Cars, 13

Tansad
"Argyle" Pedal Car, 116
"Junior" Pedal Car, 111

Tekno
Cooper Norton Racing Car, 87
DKW Junior box, 37
Ferrari Racing Sports Car, 94
Jaguar XKE Convertible, 24
Jaguar XKE Hard Top, 24
Lincoln Continental box, 37
M.G. TD Midget, 92
M.G.A. Coupé, 93
Volkswagen 1500 box, 36
Volvo Amazon 122 S, 18
Volvo Amazon Estate Car, 18
Volvo PV 544, 18

Tipp and Company, 22
Limousine, 38

"TM"
Champion Racer 301, 84

T.N.
"Hot Rod" Car, 34-35, 45
box, 34-35
New Sedan, 40
box, 35

Tomica
Mazda Savanna RL7, 77
Toyota Celica LB 2000GT, 77

Tomiyama
Firebird Racer, 84

Tootsietoy, 23

Tri-ang (Lines Brothers Ltd), 21, 25
Armstrong Siddeley 236 Sapphire, 24
Aston Martin DB3 (DB 2-4 Mk III), 92
Bristol 406, 24
"Brooklands No 8" Pedal Racing Car, 115
"Buick Regal" Pedal Car, 117
"Bullnose Morris" Pedal Car, 118
Caravan, 9
catalogue, 33
"Citroën" Pedal Car, 124
"Comet" Pedal Car, 112
Daimler Sp250 Dart, 92
"De Dion" Pedal Car, 113
Ford Saloon, 9
"Ford Zephyr" Pedal Car, 121
"Frazer Nash" Pedal Racing Car, 119
Hillman Minx box, 37
Humber Super Snipe Estate Car box, 37
Jaguar "S" Type, 24
Jaguar XKSS, 92
Jensen 541, 24
"Junior Model" Pedal Car, 110
"Magna No 8" Pedal Car, 110
M.G. Midget Mk II, 92
M.G. PB Midget (1935 Model), 92
M.G.A. Sports Car, 92
Rolls Royce, 9
Rolls Royce Electric-Powered Car, 125
Sunbeam Alpine Convertible, 92
"Vanwall" Pedal Racing Car, 123
Vauxhall Cabriolet, 9
Vauxhall Cresta, 24
Vauxhall Tourer, 9
Vauxhall Tourer Pedal Car, 124
Vauxhall Town Coupé, 9